Introduction to Photoshop

An Essential Guide for Absolute Beginners

Kevin Wilson

Apress®

Introduction to Photoshop: An Essential Guide for Absolute Beginners

Kevin Wilson
WIDNES, UK

ISBN-13 (pbk): 978-1-4842-8962-4   ISBN-13 (electronic): 978-1-4842-8963-1
https://doi.org/10.1007/978-1-4842-8963-1

Managing Director, Apress Media LLC: Welmoed Spahr
Acquisitions Editor: Celestin Suresh John
Development Editor: James Markham
Coordinating Editor: Mark Powers

Cover designed by eStudioCalamar

Cover image by Adrian Rosco on Unsplash (www.unsplash.com)

Distributed to the book trade worldwide by Apress Media, LLC, 1 New York Plaza, New York, NY 10004, U.S.A. Phone 1-800-SPRINGER, fax (201) 348-4505, e-mail orders-ny@springer-sbm.com, or visit www.springeronline.com. Apress Media, LLC is a California LLC and the sole member (owner) is Springer Science + Business Media Finance Inc (SSBM Finance Inc). SSBM Finance Inc is a **Delaware** corporation.

For information on translations, please e-mail booktranslations@springernature.com; for reprint, paperback, or audio rights, please e-mail bookpermissions@springernature.com.

Apress titles may be purchased in bulk for academic, corporate, or promotional use. eBook versions and licenses are also available for most titles. For more information, reference our Print and eBook Bulk Sales web page at http://www.apress.com/bulk-sales.

Any source code or other supplementary material referenced by the author in this book is available to readers on GitHub (https://github.com/Apress). For more detailed information, please visit http://www.apress.com/source-code.

Printed on acid-free paper

Table of Contents

About the Author

With over 20 years' experience in the computer industry, **Kevin Wilson** has made a career out of technology and showing others how to use it. After earning a master's degree in computer science, software engineering, and multimedia systems, Kevin has held various positions in the IT industry, including graphic and web design, digital film and photography, programming and software engineering, developing and managing corporate networks, building computer systems, and IT support.

He currently teaches computer science at college and works as an IT trainer in England while researching for his PhD.

Introduction

The aim of this book is to provide a first course in the use of Photoshop to manipulate and enhance photographs and create graphics for print or the Web.

It provides a foundation for those who wish to manipulate photos or create graphics based on sound design principles, and because the book is intended to be a primer, it allows the beginner to become comfortable with using Photoshop to complete various tasks.

As it is a first course, no previous experience of using Photoshop is assumed.

Throughout the book, we'll explore the ins and outs of Photoshop with practical examples and lab exercises for you to complete yourself. For this purpose, we've included various sample images and projects in the following repository: github.com/apress/introduction-to-photoshop.

CHAPTER 1

Getting Started with Photoshop

Adobe Photoshop is an image manipulation application developed by Adobe and is primarily designed for photo editing, retouching, image creation, and graphic design.

Photoshop is the industry standard and comes with a vast array of tools for manipulating digital images. It has become quite common to say that an image has been "photoshopped," meaning that it's been airbrushed, edited, or manipulated in some way.

To make full use of Photoshop you'll need a subscription to Adobe Creative Cloud. You'll then be able to download Photoshop and install it on your computer.

Creative Cloud subscriptions can be quite pricey, but you can get a Photography Package for about $20 per month which includes the latest version of Photoshop.

It should be noted that the screenshots in subsequent chapters are correct at the time of writing; however, as Adobe releases updates to Photoshop, there may be slight differences in appearance.

Let's get started.

© Kevin Wilson 2023
K. Wilson, *Introduction to Photoshop*, https://doi.org/10.1007/978-1-4842-8963-1_1

Purchasing Photoshop

You can download Photoshop from Adobe's website. Adobe apps can be quite expensive; however, you can take out a photographer's plan and use Photoshop for a fee. Open your web browser and navigate to

`www.adobe.com/creativecloud/plans.html`

Select the "Individuals" tab, then scroll down and click "Buy now" under the "Photography (1TB)" plan.

Select "Annual paid monthly," or if you want to purchase a full year, select "Annual, prepaid." Click "Buy now."

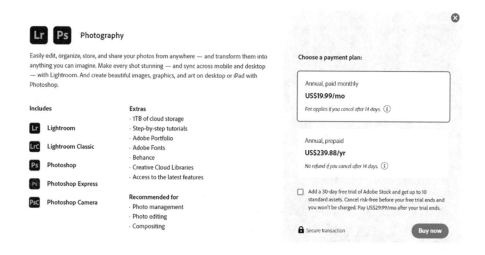

There is also a 30-day trial of Adobe Stock where you can find thousands of photos, images, and other illustrations you can use in your designs. Note that after the 30-day trial, you will be charged a fee. I usually leave this option unselected.

Enter your email address you want to use for your Adobe ID, then click "Continue" to run through the buying process.

Select your payment method: either a credit card or PayPal, enter your details, then click "Continue" or "Agree and subscribe" at the bottom of the screen.

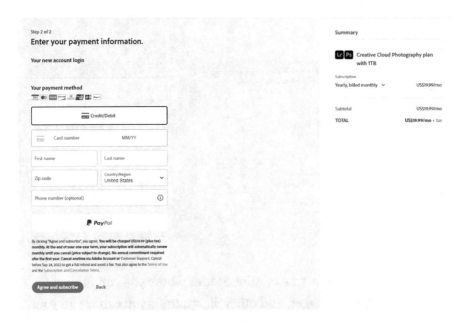

Once you've subscribed, click "Get started" to download Photoshop.

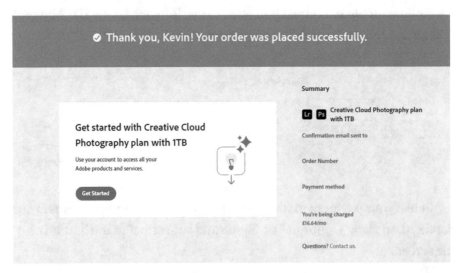

See the next section for details on how to download and install Photoshop on your computer.

Downloading Photoshop

Once you've purchased Photoshop, go to your desktop apps catalog. To do this, open your web browser, navigate to the following link:

`creativecloud.adobe.com/apps/all/desktop`

Sign in with your Adobe ID if you haven't already done so. Select all apps on the left hand side, then click on the "Desktop" tab in the middle. Scroll down to "Photoshop," then click on "Download."

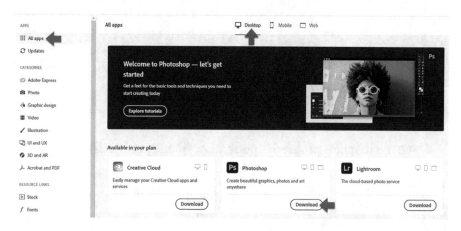

Navigate to your downloads folder using File Explorer (or Finder on a mac). Double-click the file - which is usually "Photoshop_Set-Up."

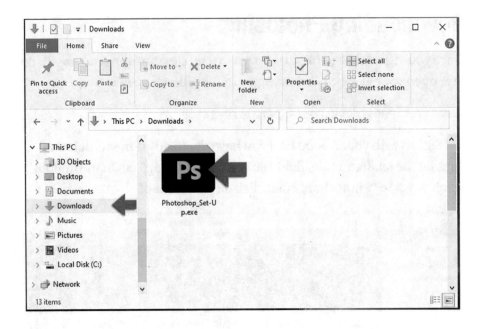

Once the installer program opens, click "Continue" on the title screen.

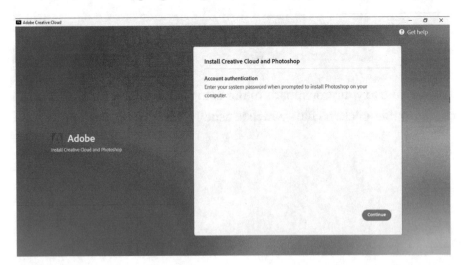

Sign in with your Adobe ID and password you created when you purchased Photoshop, click "Continue."

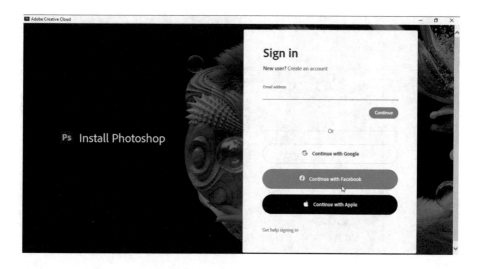

Click "Start installing" on the bottom right to run through the setup. This will take some time depending on how fast your computer is.

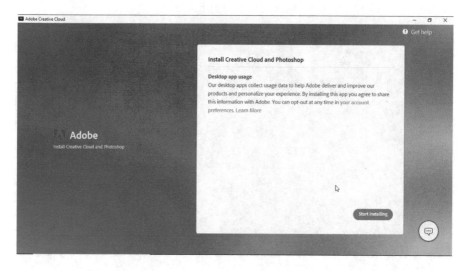

Once Creative Cloud is installed, Photoshop will follow. Allow Photoshop to install on your computer. You'll see the progress on the top right of the screen.

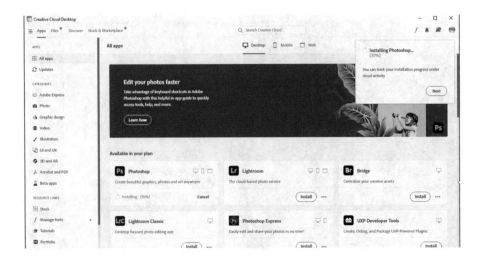

Again, this will take some time to complete.

Once installed, you'll find Adobe Photoshop on your start menu in Windows. Click the icon to launch the application.

Or if you're using a Mac, you'll find Photoshop in Finder or on Launchpad. Click the icon to launch the application.

Opening a Blank Project

Once Photoshop opens, you'll see a thumbnail list of all your most recent projects in the middle. You can either open one of these or open a new blank project.

To open a new project, click "New file" on the left-hand side of your screen. You can also select "New" from the "File" menu on the top left. Here you'll see some preset page sizes and templates.

In Figure 1-1, along the top of the "New document" dialog box, you'll see some tabs. Here you'll find preset sizes for print, art/illustration, web, and mobile. This allows you to select correct page sizes for example if you're creating a flyer that is letter size, or if you're creating a social media graphic for the web.

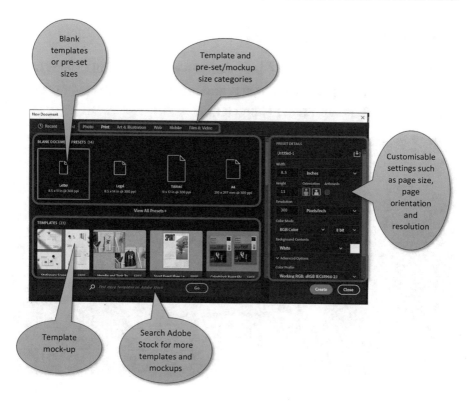

Figure 1-1. *New Document Dialog Box*

For example, if you select the "Print" tab, you'll see some familiar page sizes such as letter, legal, A4, and so on.

If we select A4, on the right-hand side you'll see the preset sizes. You can change the height and width if you need to, set the orientation to landscape, or portrait, change the resolution (300 is usually the one to go for if you're printing your work out and 72 is ideal for web). You can also set the background color (in our example, white).

Once all the settings are correct for your project, click "Create."

Photoshop will open a blank canvas for you to start your design.

Opening a Saved File

When you start Photoshop, you'll see a screen with a thumbnail view of all your most recently opened projects and images. If you see your project here, just click the thumbnail to open it up.

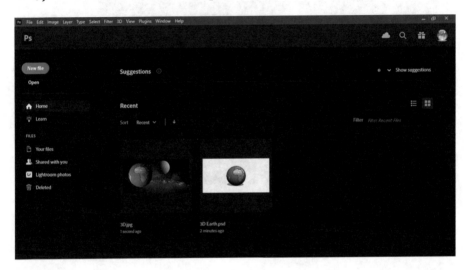

If not click "Open" on the left-hand side of your screen and browse for the project. Photoshop files have the file extension ".psd".

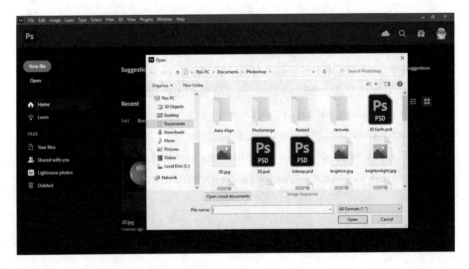

The project will open in the main window. Here you can edit and manipulate the image as you want using the various Photoshop tools

Saving a File

When saving a file in Photoshop, you have some options and file formats to consider:

- You should save your master file as a PSD – the master file is the version of your file that you want to be able to edit at the highest possible resolution/quality (usually 300dpi). This is the default and is the format that saves all the layers, effects, and edits you make to your files. To do this, use File ➤ Save As.

13

- If you're preparing your Photoshop file to send to a printing press, you'll need to use Save As. In the Save As dialog box, you can select either a TIFF, EPS, or PDF file format, depending on what the printing press requires for their printers.

- If you are saving the file to send to someone else, use in a word document, or on a website, you should export the file as a PNG or JPEG using the File ➤ Export Option, not Save As. This file doesn't save any layers and the image isn't as easily editable later on. These formats aren't as useful if you plan to edit the file as they don't preserve layer information.

Save As

To save a file, click the file menu on the top left, then select "Save as."

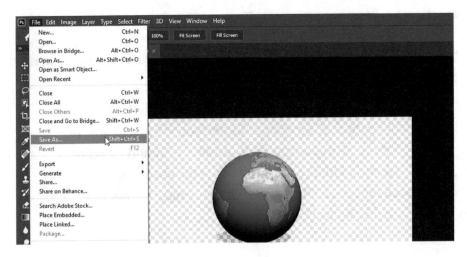

In the save as dialog box, navigate to the folder where you want to save the file, for example, in the "Pictures" folder.

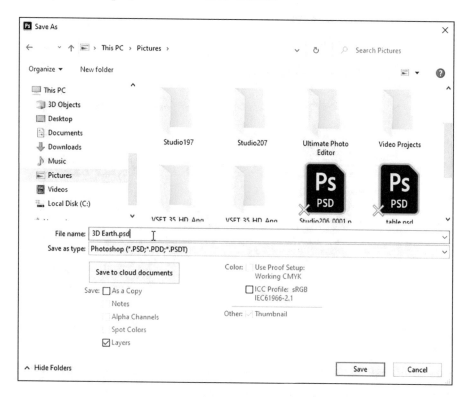

Give the file a name.

In the format dialog box, select PSD for your master high quality file you want to be able to edit later. If you are sending to a printing press, select either .TIFF, .EPS, or .PDF

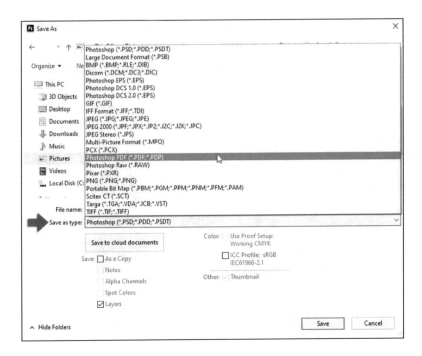

Exporting

You should use "Export As" when saving final versions of your file as a PNG or JPEG for the web, or another application such as Microsoft Word.

To do this, click the "File" menu on the top left.

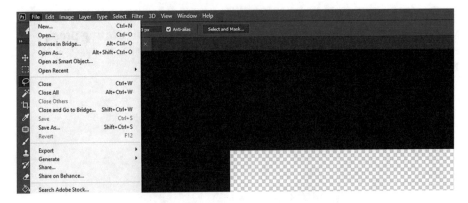

Go down to "Export." Select "Export as" from the slideout menu.

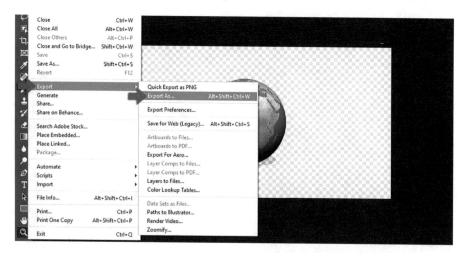

In the export dialog box, set the format to PNG or JPEG, then set the size of the image.

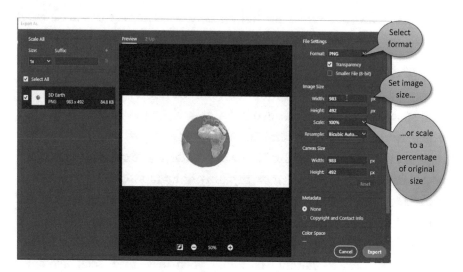

For example, set the image size width to 1000px. The height should set automatically for you in order to prevent the image from being squashed.

Click "Export."

In the "Save as" dialog box, navigate to the folder you want to export the file into. Enter a name for the file, then click "Save."

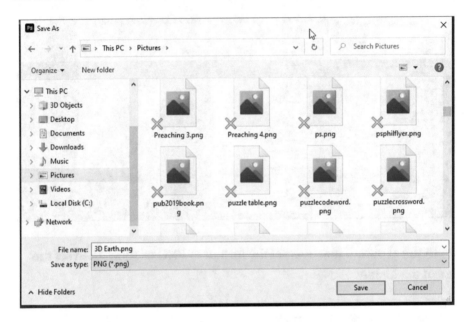

Workspaces

A workspace is a preset screen layout that sets which panels and tools are displayed on your screen and how they are arranged. Workspaces are designed to help you customize Photoshop's interface for specific tasks, to give you the tools you need. For example, a photographer will use panels and tools for image editing or retouching. A graphic designer or artist would need brushes, pens, a type tool, and color. A workspace streamlines the interface for the task at hand, removing clutter and tools you don't need to help you work more efficiently. This allows you to save the screen layout.

In this book we will be using the default workspace, but there are others such as web and graphics and photography, that reveal the panels and tools required to work on photographs and other graphics.

You can access and change the workspaces from the "Window" menu. Go down to "Workspace" and you'll find them listed.

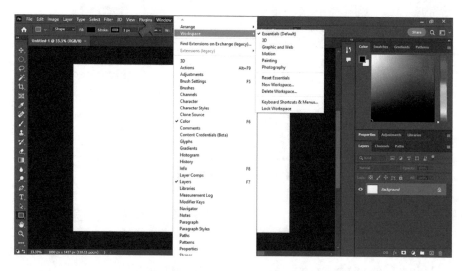

If you have moved the panels or closed ones you don't need, you can save the workspace. To do this, select "New workspace" from the slideout menu, then give it a name.

If you need to reset your workspace, perhaps some panels have vanished, you can do this using the "Reset workspace" option.

Cancelling a Subscription

Once you sign up with Adobe Creative Cloud to use Photoshop, you'll be charged a monthly fee until cancelled, whether you use the application or not. So if you no longer want to use Photoshop, you'll need to cancel the subscription.

Open your web browser and navigate to

`account.adobe.com/plans`

Select "Manage plan" for the plan you want to cancel.

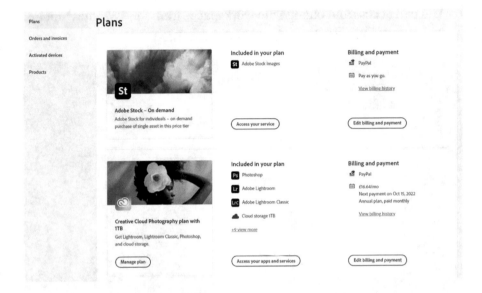

Select Cancel your plan next to "End your service."

Indicate the reason for cancellation, and then select Continue.

Lab Exercises

1. Download and install Photoshop on your machine if you haven't already done so.

2. Practice opening files from templates or files that have been previously saved.

3. How do you save a file?

4. When should you use "Save as"?

5. When should you use "Export"?

6. Name some image file formats.

Summary

- Adobe Photoshop is an image manipulation application used for photo retouching, image creation, and graphic design and is developed by Adobe Inc. for Windows and macOS.

- Available from Adobe.com

- We learned how to open a new Photoshop file.

- Use "Save as" to PSD for your master, high quality file you want to be able to edit later.

- Use "Export as" to export files as PNG or JPEG for the web or other apps such as Word.

- Use .PDF, .EPS, or .TIFF if saving files for commercial printing press.

- A workspace is a preset screen layout that sets which panels and tools are displayed on your screen and how they are arranged.

CHAPTER 2

Getting around Photoshop

In this chapter, we'll take a look around the Photoshop interface and how to use the most common tools to manipulate and edit photographs.

Photoshop has a vast array of tools and can appear quite overwhelming at first, but in this chapter, we'll explore what the various tools do and how to use them.

Let's start by taking a look at the main screen.

The Main Screen Overview

At the very top of the screen, you'll see Photoshop's drop-down menu system. Here, you'll find options to open files, save files, copy, paste, image adjustments, as well as type options, filters, and so on. Just click the appropriate menu along the bar, then select the option you want.

© Kevin Wilson 2023
K. Wilson, *Introduction to Photoshop*, https://doi.org/10.1007/978-1-4842-8963-1_2

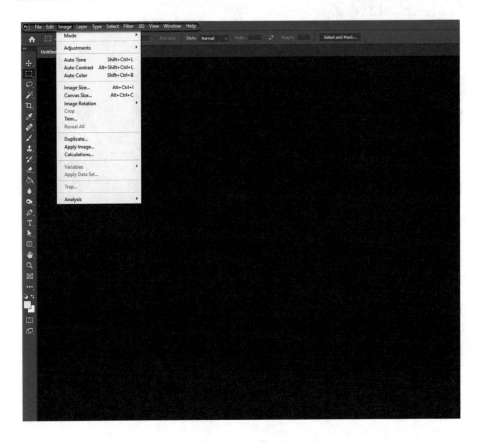

Underneath the menus, you'll see the options bar. This bar changes depending on which tool is selected from the toolbox (sometimes called the toolbar or tools panel). It allows you to change brush size, text size, color, and so on.

Along the left-hand side of your screen is the tool box. This is where you'll find all your tools, the paint brush, eraser, pen tool, text tool, crop tool, and so on.

Right at the bottom of your tool box, you can select foreground color - this is the color of your paint brush, text, shape, and anything you draw. The background color is the color of the background layer, the color of the eraser tool and the end color of a gradient (gradients go from foreground to background color).

In the following illustration, the foreground color is black and the background color is white. The double-sided arrow on the top right swaps the colors around.

The Toolbox and Options Bar

In the Photoshop window, the toolbox appears on the left of the screen. As you can see, Photoshop has an enormous array of tools available. Many of these tools also have options that appear in the options bar at the top of the screen.

For example, if I select the horizontal text tool from the toolbox on the left-hand side, as we can see in the following screenshot.

Along the top of the screen, I have some options I can change, such as font, size, color, alignment, and so on.

Just click the option you want to change. For example, if you wanted to change the font, click the first drop-down box ('arial' in the following example), then select a font from the list. If you want to change the font size, click the font size drop-down box (currently set to 19pt in the following example), then select or type in a size.

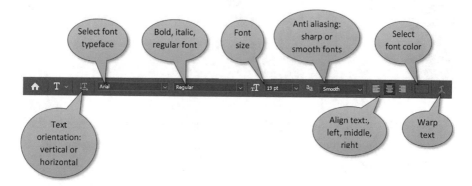

Similarly, if I selected the brush tool from the toolbox on the left-hand side.

From the options bar along the top of the screen, you can change the brush size using the brush preset drop-down. You can also change the hardness and softness of the brush.

Try different brush sizes, change the hardness, and see what happens.

Along the top of the options bar, I can also change the opacity, the flow rate (how fast or how much "paint" comes out), and the smoothing (helps smooth out your brush strokes).

The options bar will display the options related to the tool selected from the toolbox. Try out some of the settings on the text tool and paintbrush tools.

Give it a try, see what happens when you select different opacity, and flow settings.

Additional related tools are indicated by a small arrow at the bottom right of the tool icon.

If you click a tool and hold your mouse button down for a second, you'll see these additional tools.

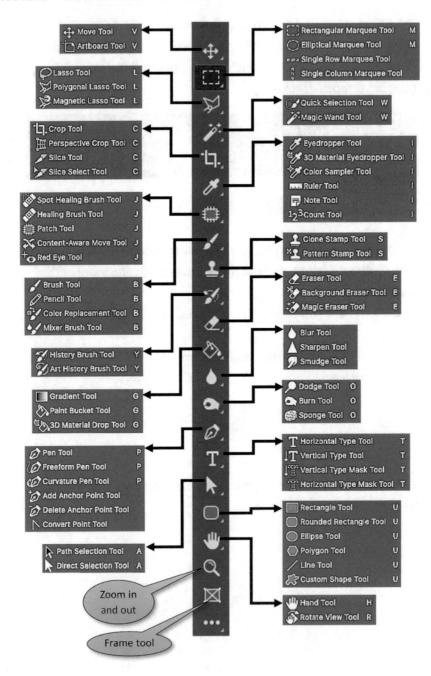

At the bottom of the toolbox, you can change the foreground and background colors. The foreground color is applied to painting, drawing, and text tools to set the color of that object. Background color is applied with the eraser tool and is the end color of a gradient.

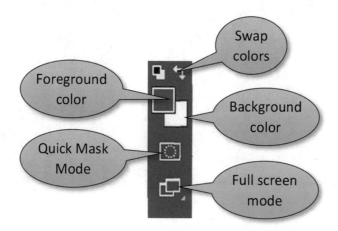

Let's explore the most commonly used tools.

Move Tool

Once an area of an image is highlighted with the rectangular marquee tool, the move tool can be used to manually relocate the selected piece to anywhere on the canvas.

Marquee Tools

The marquee tools can make selections that are single row, single column, rectangular, and elliptical.

An area that has been selected can be edited without affecting the rest of the image. Once you've selected the tool, click and drag your mouse across the desired area to select it. The selected area will be outlined by dotted lines, referred to as "marching ants."

Lasso Tool

The lasso tool is similar to the marquee tool; however, you can make a custom selection by drawing it freehand. There are three lasso tools – regular, polygonal, and magnetic.

The regular lasso tool allows you to trace around your selection freehand. Photoshop will complete the selection once the mouse button is released. You can also complete the selection by connecting the end point to the starting point. The "marching ants" will indicate if a selection has been made.

The polygonal lasso tool will only draw straight lines, which makes it an ideal choice for images with many straight lines. Unlike the regular lasso tool, you must continually click around the image to outline the shape. To complete the selection, you must connect the end point to the starting point just like the regular lasso tool.

Magnetic lasso tool is considered a smart tool. It can do the same as the other two, but it can also detect the edges of an image once the user selects a starting point. It detects the edge of an object by examining difference in pixels as the cursor moves over the desired area. Closing the selection is the same as the other two, which should also display the "marching ants" once the selection has been closed.

Quick Selection Tool

The quick selection tool selects areas based on edges, similarly to the magnetic lasso tool.

The difference between this tool and the lasso tool is that there is no starting and ending point. Since there isn't a starting and ending point, the selected area can be added on to as much as possible without starting over.

By dragging the cursor over the desired area, the quick selection tool detects the edges of the image. The "marching ants" tell you what is currently being selected. Once done, the selected area can be edited without affecting the rest of the image.

Magic Wand

The magic wand tool selects areas based on pixels of a similar color and intensity. You only need to click once, and this tool will detect pixels that are very similar to each other. When the image requires more than a few clicks, this tool doesn't work particularly well.

Crop Tool

The crop tool can be used to select a particular area of an image and discard the portions outside of the chosen section.

A crop creates a focal point on an image, excluding unnecessary or excess space. Click and drag the cursor around the desired area, hit enter and the area outside of the rectangle is discarded.

Slice Tool

The slice tool is used in isolating parts of an image. The slice tool can be used to divide an image into different sections, and these separate parts can be used as pieces of a web page.

The slice select tool allows sliced sections of an image to be adjusted and shifted.

Eye Dropper

You can use the eye dropper tool to sample a color on an image, layer, or object.

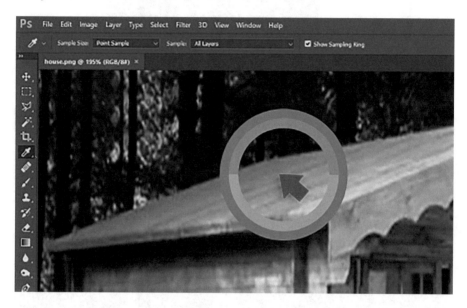

Click and hold your mouse on a particular color you want to sample, and you'll see the sample ring. The outside color is a neutral grey which is meant to help you distinguish the colors. On the inner ring, the top half is the color you just sampled, and the bottom half is the previous color you sampled. Your sampled color will appear as the foreground color on the bottom of your toolbox.

Healing Brush

The healing brush allows you to fix image imperfections such as scratches or blemishes by sampling the surrounding area or using a predefined pattern.

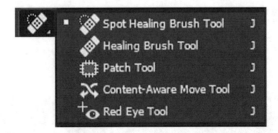

You can blend the imperfections into the rest of the image.

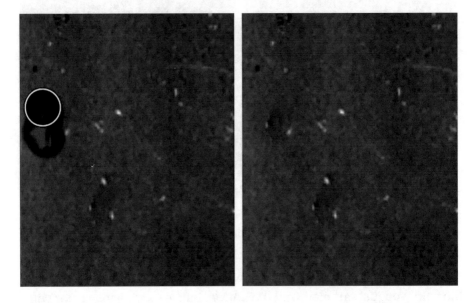

Patch Tool

The patch tool is used to repair larger areas of an image or remove any unwanted objects or blemishes. The idea is, you draw around the bit you want to patch, then drag the selection onto a clean area of the image.

This will copy the clean area onto the bit you selected, patching it up.

Pencils and Brushes

The pencil and brush tools allow you to draw freehand illustrations and make minor touch ups to images.

Select the paint brush tool from the tool box. You can change the size, shape, and hardness of the brush on the options bar at the top of the screen.

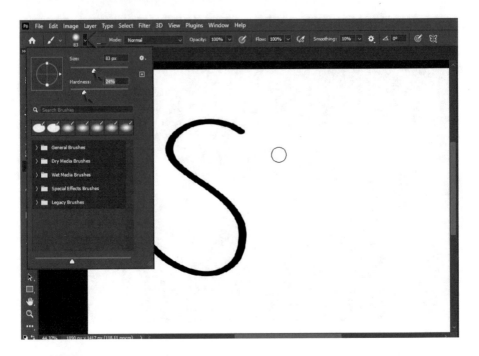

Size is the thickness of the brush, while hardness is how much the brush feathers at the edges.

Soft brush   **Hard brush**

Change the color of the brush using the color selector at the bottom of the toolbox on the left-hand side.

You can change the shape of the brush too. Open the brush panel from the options bar and on the top left, drag the two small white dots on the brush to change the shape.

Underneath that you can select some preset brush styles. These are grouped into folders according to their type. Browse through the folders and try out some of the brushes.

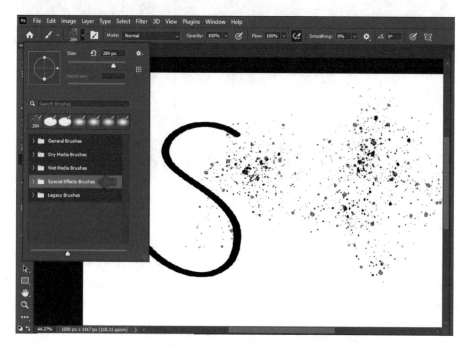

There are some general brushes and also some special effect brushes. You can also use the "Search brushes" field to search.

Select one, then draw directly onto the canvas with your brush.

Try some of them out, see what happens.

A good accessory to use when drawing freehand is a graphics tablet or a laptop/tablet with a touch screen. You can run the Photoshop app on an iPad, or you can use Photoshop on a touchscreen PC. You can download Photoshop from the app store on your iPad or tablet.

Clone Stamp Tool

The clone stamp tool samples a selected portion of an image and duplicates it over another area using a brush that can be adjusted in size, flow, and opacity.

Useful for "airbrushing" small parts of an image. If part of an original image is damaged, the damaged area can be restored by cloning a similar area from within the same image. This tool works great for removing unwanted blemishes.

Hold down the Alt key (or option if you're on a mac), then click the area to sample. Select an area that is similar to the one you want to fix.

Once the sample area has been cloned, click the area of the photo to be edited - use the tool like a paint brush and "paint" over the blemishes.

You can change the size and softness of the brush using the tools along the top of the screen.

Smudge

The smudge tool smudges the image when dragged over as if it was watercolor paint.

Here you can see an example of how the flower petal is smudged

Blur

The blur tool softens portions of an image by blurring the area.

Here you can see an example of how the flower petal is blurred

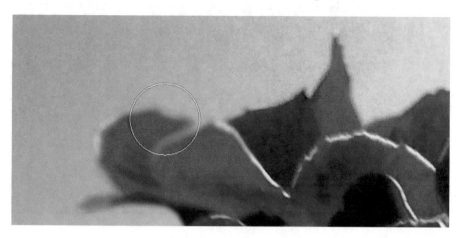

Burn and Dodge

The burn and dodge tools, which are derived from traditional methods of adjusting the exposure on printed photos, have opposite effects.

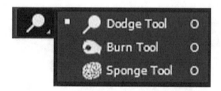

The burn tool darkens selected areas, and the dodge tool lightens them.

Eraser

The eraser tool will convert the pixels to transparent unless it is the background layer. The size and style of the eraser can be selected in the options bar.

This tool is unique in that it can take the form of the paintbrush and pencil tools. In addition to the straight eraser tool, there are two more available options – background eraser and magic eraser. The background eraser deletes any part of the image that is on the edge of an object. This tool is often used to extract objects from the background.

The magic eraser tool deletes based on similar colored pixels. It is very similar to the magic wand tool.

This tool is ideal for deleting areas with the same color or tone that contrasts with the rest of the image.

Pen Tool

The pen tool creates precise paths that can be manipulated using anchor points.

Here you can see we've added some anchor points around the edge of the boat.

Text Tool

The text tool creates an area on a new layer where text can be entered. Use the options bar along the top of the screen to change font, size, alignment, and color. There are two types, horizontal and vertical.

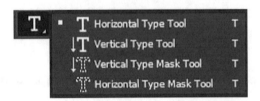

Here we've added some text using the horizontal text tool.

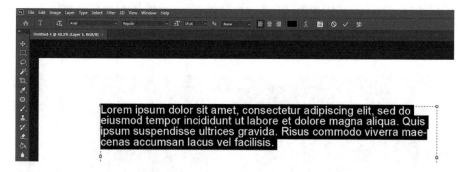

Shapes

The shapes tool allows you to create different types of shapes such as squares, rectangles, and ellipses, as well as polygons with three sides or more such as triangles, pentagons, hexagons, and so on.

Select the polygon tool, it's on the shapes tool - click and hold your mouse button on the icon on the toolbox for a second to reveal the menu. From this menu, you can select a standard square/rectangle, ellipse, or polygon. For this example, I'm going to select "Polygon tool."

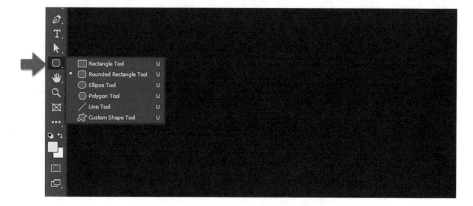

Notice in the options bar at the top of the screen, you can change the fill color as well as the number of sides your polygon has. In this example, I'm going to add a pentagon. This shape has five sides, so enter 5 into "sides" field.

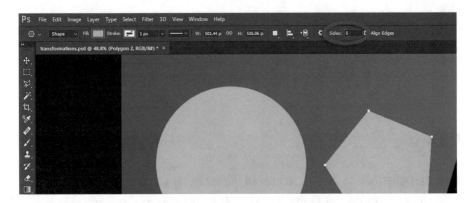

Click on the canvas, then drag your mouse to size the shape.

You can change the fill color and outline (stroke). To do this, click the fill box on the left-hand side of the options bar, then select a color. Do the same for stroke. Click the drop-down box to the left to change the outline thickness (or stroke).

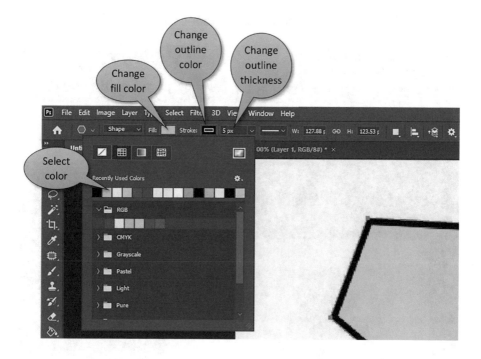

Give it a try.

Custom Shapes

Photoshop also has some custom shapes such as arrows and decorative shapes you can use.

From the shapes tool on the toolbox, click and hold your mouse for a second to reveal the menu. Select "Custom shapes tool."

Click the custom shape icon on the options bar on the top right.

Open the folders underneath, then select a shape from the options.

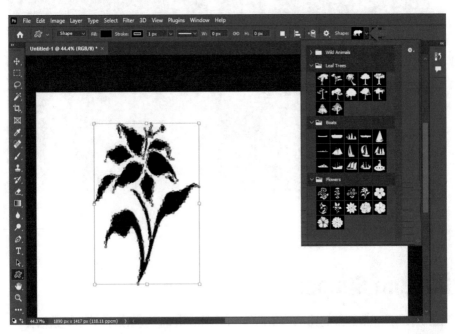

Click and drag your mouse on the canvas to create your shape. To maintain the shape's aspect ratio, hold down the shift key while you click and drag your mouse on the canvas to create your shape - this prevents the shape from being stretched or squashed.

Panels

You can find your panels displayed down the right-hand side of your screen. These panels contain adjustments and customizations for your tools. The default layout will look similar to the following ones.

There is a panel for adjustments and controlling color, a panel for character styles, text alignment, and fonts. There is also a panel for managing layers and properties of objects among many others.

The panels are anchored to the panel dock on the right-hand side of the screen, but you can move them around if you need to.

Opening and Closing Panels

Most tools have a panel with adjustments and customizations, but they don't all open up at the same time. You can open additional panels from the "Window" menu.

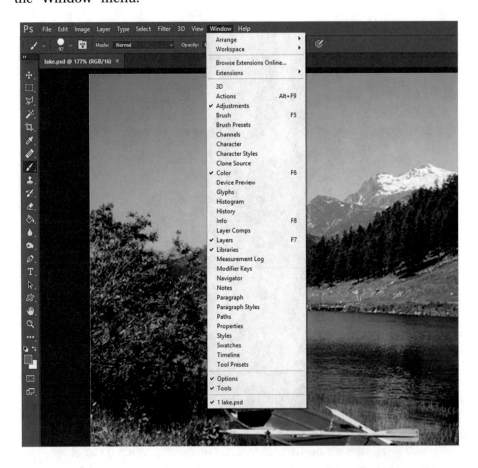

Panels that are currently open will have a tick next to the name in the "Window" menu.

If you need to close a panel, right click the tab, select close from the popup menu

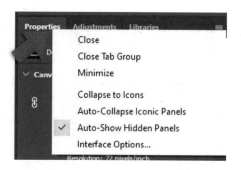

Layers Panel

One of the most important panels is the layers panel. On some workspaces, this doesn't always show up.

To reveal the layers panel, click the "Window" menu, then select "Layers."

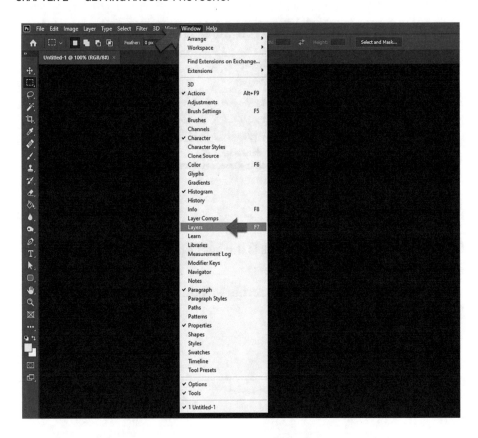

You'll see the panel open up on the right-hand side.

The layers panel is where you'll build up your design, graphic, collage, and effects in your projects.

Let's have a look at the different parts of the layers panel.

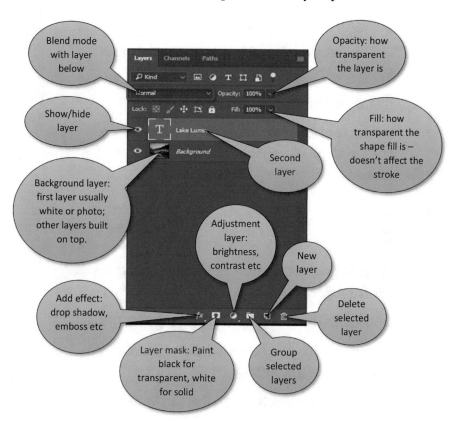

We'll take a closer look at layers in more detail later in this book, but for now, familiarize yourself with the icons on the panel and what they do.

Lab Exercises

1. Open a new A4 Photoshop document.

2. Use the text tool to add some text.

3. Make the text larger.

4. Change the text color to red.

5. Change the font typeface.

6. Use the paint brush tool to draw a picture below the text.

7. Change the brush size and color.

8. Take note of the layers panel as you add your text and drawings. What happens? What layers are created?

Summary

- Photoshop tools are available from the toolbox on the left-hand side.

- Options for tools show up along the top of the screen.

- Click and hold your mouse pointer on a tool on the toolbox to open more tools.

- Pen tool creates precise paths that can be manipulated using anchor points.

- Crop tool can be used to select a particular area of an image and discard the portions outside of the chosen section.

- The slice tool is used in isolating parts of an image to be used on a website.

- The move or marquee tool is used to manually relocate the selected piece to anywhere on the canvas.

- Lasso tool is similar to the marquee tool; however, you can make a custom selection by drawing it freehand.

- Quick selection tool selects areas based on edges, similarly to the magnetic lasso tool.

- The magic wand tool selects areas based on pixels of a similar color and intensity.

- The eraser tool will convert the pixels to transparent unless it is the background layer.

- The text tool creates an area on a new layer where text can be entered.

- Clone stamp tool samples a selected portion of an image and duplicates it over another area using a brush that can be adjusted in size, flow, and opacity.

- Custom shapes allow you to create different types of shapes such as squares, rectangles, and ellipses, as well as polygons with three sides or more such as triangles, pentagons, hexagons, and so on.

- Pencils and brushes allow you to draw freehand illustrations and make minor touch ups to images.

- You can use the eye dropper tool to sample a color on an image, layer, or object.

- The layers panel is where you'll build up your design, collage, and effects in your projects.

CHAPTER 3

Basic Skills

In this chapter, we'll be looking at performing some common tasks using Photoshop. We'll have a look at how to import images from scanners or cameras, as well as crop, resize, image manipulation, batch processing, and various other things you can do with Photoshop.

For these examples, you'll need to download the Photoshop resources. Download and unpack the zip file into your pictures folder.

github.com/apress/introduction-to-photoshop

Import Images

You can import images from a variety of sources:

- Scanners
- Digital cameras

You'll need to connect your scanner or camera to your computer using a USB cable.

© Kevin Wilson 2023
K. Wilson, *Introduction to Photoshop*, https://doi.org/10.1007/978-1-4842-8963-1_3

Figure 3-1. *USB Scanner Connected to a PC*

Open Photoshop. From the file menu, select import, then click "WIA support" ("Images from Device" if you're on a Mac). In the following example, I'm importing an image from my scanner.

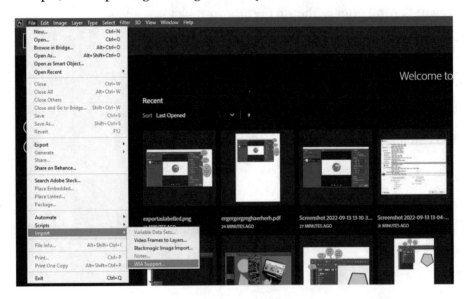

Change the destination folder if you need to, then click "Start."

Select your scanning device from the options, then click OK.

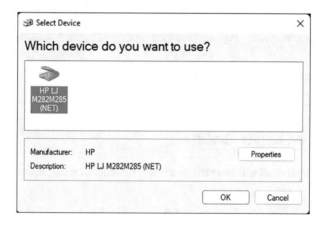

When the scanner window appears, select color picture. If you want to change the settings such as use a different resolution - 150dpi or 300dpi - click custom settings.

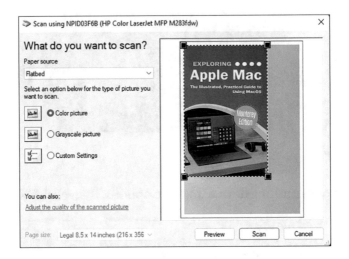

Click "Scan" when you're done.

Change Image Size

The image size menu allows you to view and adjust pixel information, document size, and resolution.

The following example uses the **flower.jpg** file in your pictures folder.

Click the image menu then select "Image size."

To adjust image size, you can adjust the pixel dimensions in this dialog box. This picture is 1920 pixels by 2560 pixels.

Keeping the "Constrain proportions" icon checked allows you to change either the width or height of the image while maintaining the proportionate size of the picture (the aspect ratio).

If it's easier, you can also change the picture size at a percentage by changing the pixels drop-down box to percentage. You can also select centimeters or inches if you prefer. Click OK.

Photoshop will resample the image.

Rotate an Image

Sometimes photos need to be rotated; perhaps you took a photo in portrait mode, as shown in the following, but has been imported "sideways." It is easy to rotate and flip images in Photoshop.

Go to the image menu and select "Image Rotation."

You can rotate your images using some presets, these are:

- 180° (rotates image 180°)

- 90° CW (rotates clockwise - as in the preceding example)

- 90° CCW (rotates counter-clockwise)

- Arbitrary – lets you choose the angle, for example, 45°

Also you can mirror image your photos or images by flipping them horizontally or vertically. These work great for creating reflection effects.

Flip Horizontally   Flip Vertically

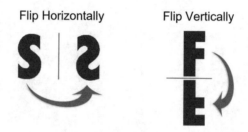

Crop an Image

Use the crop tool to crop an image or photo. This can improve the appearance of your image by re-framing or removing unwanted parts of a photo, as well as decrease the file size.

For this example, we will use **molly.jpg**

From the toolbox, select the crop tool.

Select the area you wish to keep by clicking and dragging the highlighted rectangle around the area. Notice how the area you want to keep is highlighted, but the area to be discarded is darkened.

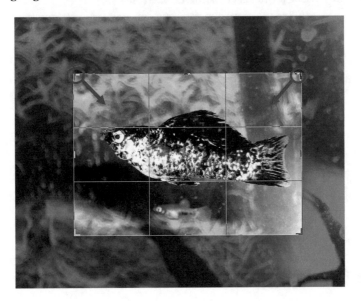

To resize the crop box, click and drag the corners around the area you want to keep.

Double-click the center of the highlighted area. This removes the area outside of the crop box.

Content Aware Crop

Content aware fills the areas outside the original image when you perform a reverse crop. Photoshop will make a best guess based on the background of your image.

Select the crop tool from the toolbox on the left-hand side. Along the bar at the top, you'll see an option called "Content Aware." Click the tick box next to the option to enable it.

Now drag the corner crop handle outwards to enlarge the crop. Hit the tick icon on the bar at the top to execute the crop.

See how Photoshop has continued the background pattern on the image on the right.

Adjust an Image

Under the image menu, there is a slideout menu called "Adjustments." This menu has several adjustment controls that can improve the look and feel of your image.

For this exercise, open **daffodils.jpg**

Go to the image menu, select "Adjustments," and then click "Levels."

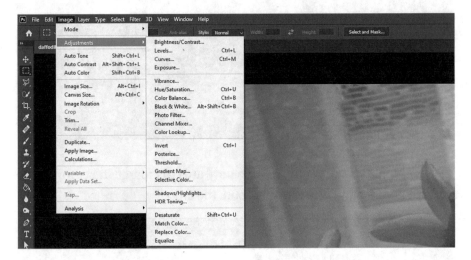

Click "Auto" in the levels dialog box. Photoshop now will analyze the image and adjust the color, contrast, and color balance for you.

Auto levels changes the brightness, contrast, color setting, highlights, and shadows.

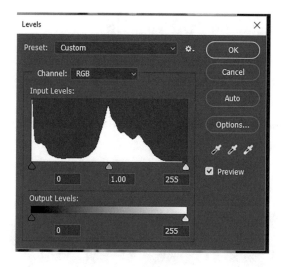

Sometimes the auto adjust doesn't always get it right. You can manually adjust the image with the histogram sliders marked as follows.

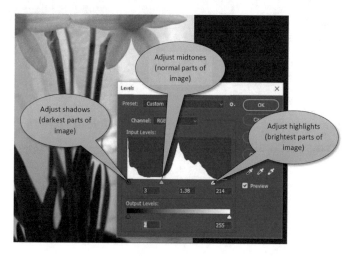

Move some of the sliders and see what happens. What happens when you move the left-hand slider slightly to the right? What about the middle slider? What happens when you move the right hand slider to the left? Click "OK" when you're done.

Hue and Saturation levels

We can also adjust the image using the hue/saturation levels. This adjusts the tint, intensity, and brightness of your colors. For example, lets change the color of the daffodils.

Open the **daffodils.jpg** image and save it as a Photoshop file (PSD) in your pictures folder.

Open the hue/saturation window under the images/adjustments menu.

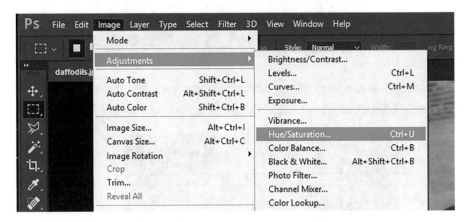

In the popup dialog box, move the hue slider left or right to change the hue of the image. How about purple daffodils?

Experiment with the different settings. What happens when you move the saturation and lightness sliders?

Click where it says "Master." You can change the hue of the reds or greens in the photograph and move the Hue Saturation and Lightness sliders for those channels as well. Give it a try. Click OK when you're done.

Brightness and Contrast

The brightness/contrast tool is extremely useful for making adjustments to the lighting.

Open the **brighton.jpg** image.

Go to image menu and select "Adjustments." From the slideout, select "Brightness/Contrast."

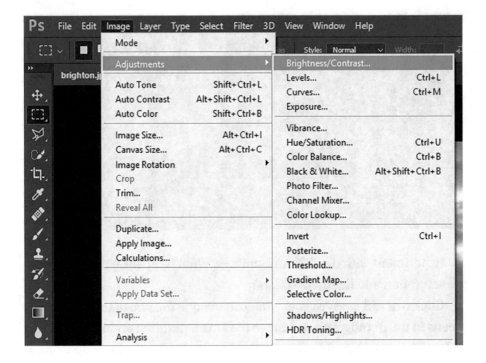

Move the brightness slider to the right to lighten the picture.

Move the contrast slider to the left to add back some of the picture's detail in the shadows.

Try different settings and see what happens. Click OK when you're done.

Shadows and Highlights

There is another way to adjust picture brightness that may work better for photos with underexposed areas. Under the Image/Adjustments menu, there is an option called Shadows/Highlights. This option allows you to lighten areas that are dark due to shadows and add back some detail in the brighter parts of the images.

To work with these tools, let's open **brighton.jpg**.

Go to the image menu, select "Adjustments." From the slideout menu select "Shadows/Highlights." Photoshop now will open a dialog box and automatically reduce shadows by 50%. Note that if you cannot see all settings, make sure that the "Show more options" checkbox is enabled.

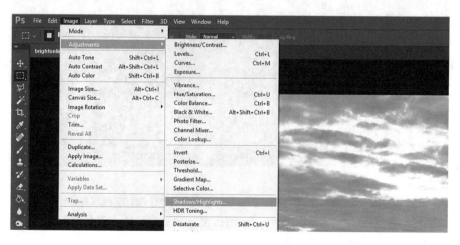

We can change the amount of shadow by moving the slider left or right. Moving the slider completely to the right removes 100% of the shadows. Notice the additional detail on the road. At the same time, the sky remains cloudy, rather than being bright and washed out as when only using the brightness control.

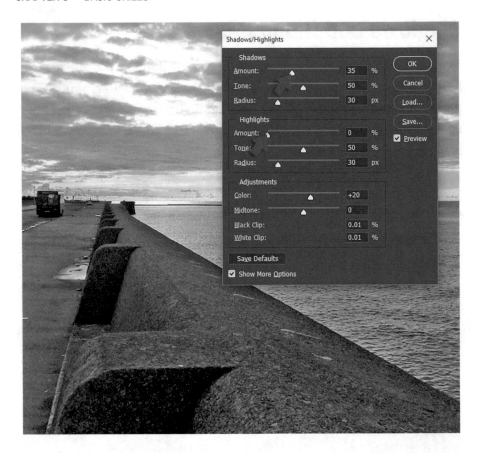

The highlight control allows you to darken and bring out some of the detail in the brighter parts of the picture as you move the slider to the right. Use these controls sparingly.

Curves

The curves tool allows you to control shadows, highlights, and midtones separately. This is called the tonal range.

Open **brighton.jpg**

From the image menu, go down to "adjustments" select "Curves."

In the dialog box, you'll see a graph appear. The graph is split into sections. The first section on the left is blacks and shadows. This is the darkest areas in the image. The two sections in the middle are mid tones and highlights such as the brighter parts of the image usually the sky.

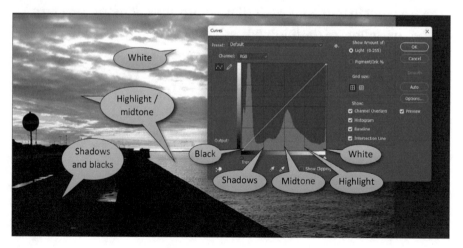

The graph indicates the amount of each of these values. For example, in the preceding image, there is a lot of shadow and black on the bottom left. If you look at the graph you'll see a spike showing the amount of shadow.

If you click an area in the image, you can see where they appear on the histogram

Moving a point at the top of the line adjusts the highlights, whereas moving a point in the center of the line adjusts the midtones. Moving a point at the bottom of the line adjusts the shadows.

To adjust these levels, we move the diagonal white line going through the middle. Try to drag the middle point upwards.

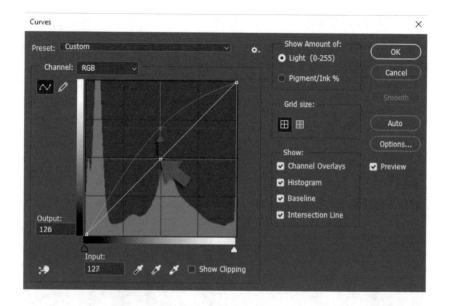

When you do this, you'll notice a point appear and the line will curve. Try bringing up the shadows in the dark area.

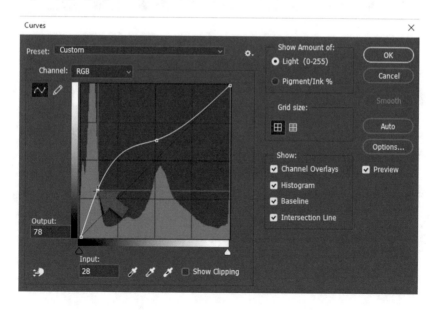

Experiment with adding different points on the curve. Try adjusting the sky. What happens when you move the very end point on the blacks or whites?

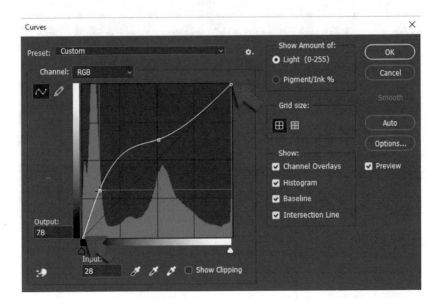

See what happens to the image.

Free Transform Tool

The free transform tool allows you to resize, distort or rotate an image, object, or shape on a particular layer.

For this exercise, open up **transformations.psd**

You can transform any object or image. To do this, make sure you have selected the layer that the image or object is on in the layers panel on the right-hand side. In this example, select the Screen layer.

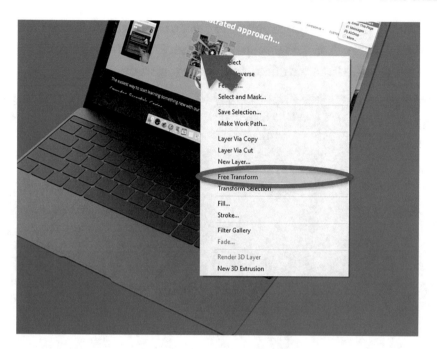

Once you have done that, select the rectangular marquee tool from your tool box.

Click and drag the box around the object, then right click your mouse on the selection. From the popup menu, select "Free Transform," or alternatively use from the edit menu, select transform.

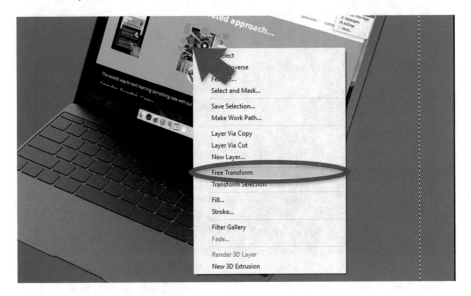

Now, you'll notice some resize handles appear around the selection. Click and drag these to resize your object. In this example, I am making the laptop image smaller.

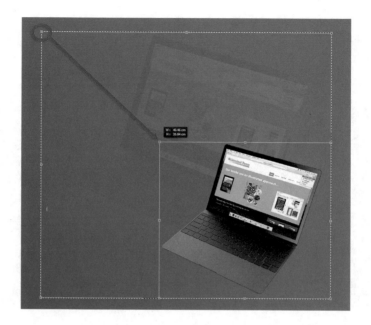

You can also rotate the image. To do this, hover your mouse around one of the corners of the selection. When the cursor becomes a double curved arrow, click and drag the resize handle in the direction you want to rotate the image - you'll see a gauge appear with the number of degrees rotated.

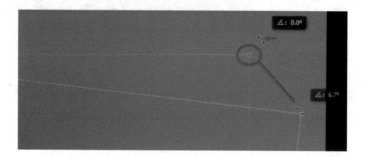

If you right click your selection again, you'll see a transform menu. This has some preset functions such as distort, perspective, and so on.

Try out some of these options. Try "Warp," "Skew," "Distort," or "Perspective," and see what they do.

Press enter on your keyboard, or click the tick on the top right of the options bar to execute the transform.

Using Brushes

The brush tool allows you to paint on the canvas. Open a blank file, then select the brush tool from the toolbox on the left-hand side.

Using the options bar along the top, you can select the brush size and softness.

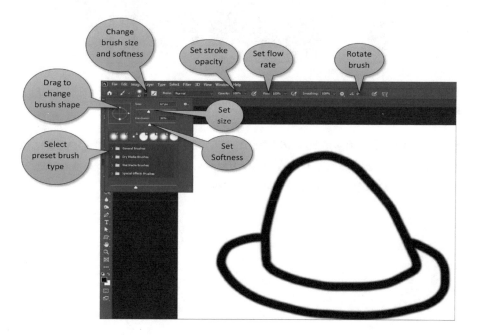

Once you know how to use the Brush tool, you'll notice that many other tools, including the Eraser and the Spot Healing Brush, use a similar group of settings.

To change the color of the brush, double-click your foreground color in the toolbox. Then, in the Color Picker dialog box, select a color. Click OK when you're done.

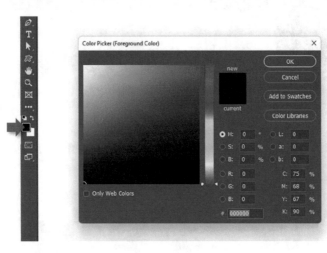

Adding Text

The text tool allows you to add text to your image. For example, if you were creating a poster, greeting card, or invitation. To add text, select the text tool from the toolbox on the left-hand side.

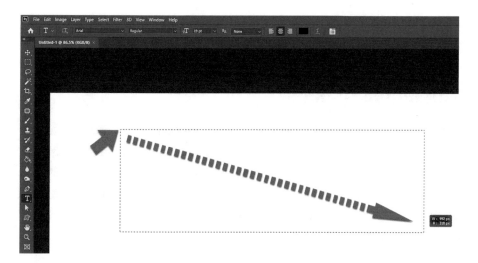

Click and drag your mouse across the canvas to add the textbox. Replace the default text with your own.

Highlight the text, then use the options bar to change the font size and typeface, as well as the text alignment.

To change the color, select the text, then use the color selector on the options bar along the top.

Select a color from the Color Picker dialog box. Click OK when you're done.

Automated Actions

Automated actions allow you to record and execute tasks automatically. This is useful for processing multiple images when you need to apply the same steps to each image, or when you need to automatically build a Photoshop project such as a book cover template or a product mockup, shown as follows, that would only need the artwork changing rather than the whole design and layout.

The action feature will record each step you take to process your photograph or project which can be "replayed" later.

Perhaps you want to resize or crop a whole load of high resolution photos from your favorite DSLR camera to email to friends, post on social media or use on a website. It would be very time-consuming to do them all manually.

In this example, I'm going to resize the photos to make them easier to send to people. Open the image **clownloachhighres.jpg**.

The list of steps in this procedure are

1.   Image ➤ Image Size

2. Set width to 1024 pixels

3. Set resolution to 300dpi

4. Click OK

5. File ➤ Save As

To create a new action, click the "Window" menu and select "Actions." This will open the actions panel on the right-hand side.

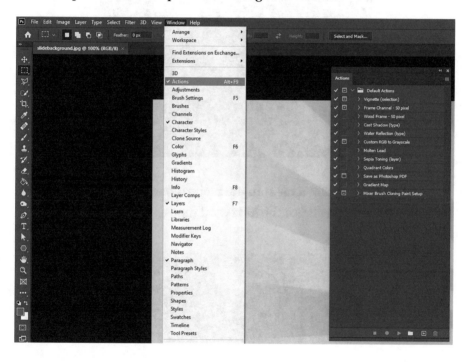

Click the "new action" icon on the bottom right of the panel.

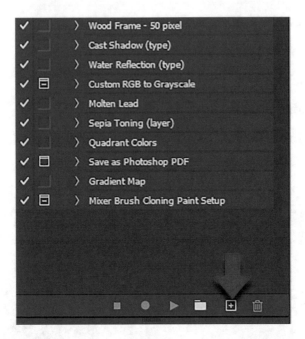

Give your new action a meaningful name when prompted then click "Record." Photoshop will now be in Record mode.

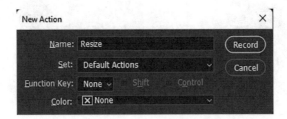

Any action you take in Photoshop will now be recorded. This is where you can now run through the procedure or steps you want to record in your "Action."

Now we need to run through the procedure to resize the image. From the "Image" menu, select "Image Size."

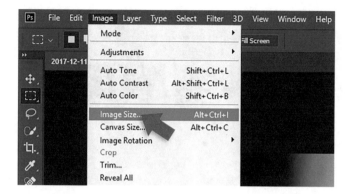

Set the resolution to 300dpi, make sure the aspect ratio lock is enabled between the width and height, then adjust the width to 1024 pixels. Click OK.

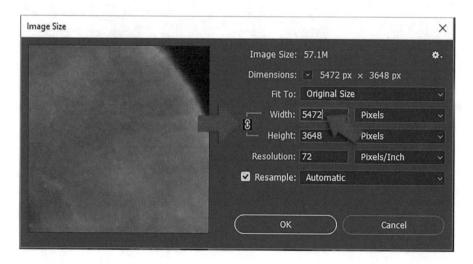

Next, we want to save the processed image. So click the "File" menu then select "Save as."

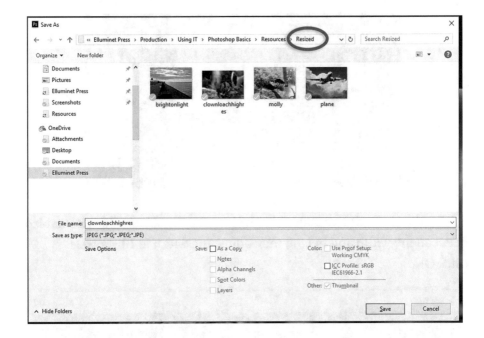

Create a new folder called "Resized" and save the processed image in there. *On a Windows machine, just right click and select new folder from the popup menu. Click "New Folder" if you're on a Mac.*

In the "Save as" drop-down, select either jpg or png.

Click the stop icon on the bottom of the actions panel. You'll see your action added to the actions panel.

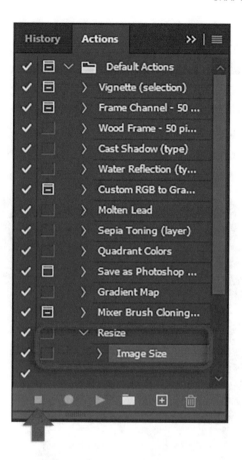

To run the action, you can open any image and execute the action and it will resize any image to 1024 pixels (as we resized during recording). To do this, click the action "Image Size," then click the "play" icon.

Notice that this only works with one image... What happens if we had 1000 images to resize? This is where batch processing comes in. We'll look at that next.

Batch Processing

Batch processing allows you to automate actions when you have a lot of images to process.

You can find the batch processing on the file menu.

File ➤ Automate ➤ Batch.

From the top left of the dialog box, select your action. In this example, I'm going to use the resize action we created in the previous section.

Click "Choose," then select the source folder where your images have been saved. In this example, I am resizing some photos I saved in my pictures folder from my DSLR camera.

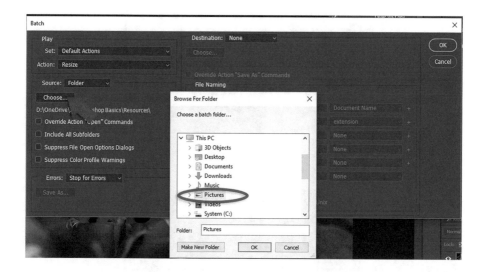

Change the destination drop-down menu to "folder." This is where you want to save the resized images.

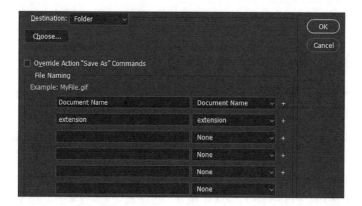

Click "choose," then browse and select the folder from the popup window. It makes sense to save these into a separate folder. I'm going to save them in to a folder called "Resized." If the folder doesn't exist, click "Make New Folder." Click "OK" when you're done.

You can use the batch processing feature to run any of the actions as well as ones you've recorded yourself.

Printing Images

Most of the time you'll probably print images using a desktop printer, such as a laser or inkjet. If this is the case, make sure you use RGB mode when printing to a desktop printer, as these printers are configured to accept RGB images and will convert to CMYK. If you send CMYK images, most desktop printers will assume its RGB and apply a conversion anyway producing unexpected results. More on RGB and CMYK in Chapter 9.

To print your image, go up to the file menu and select print.

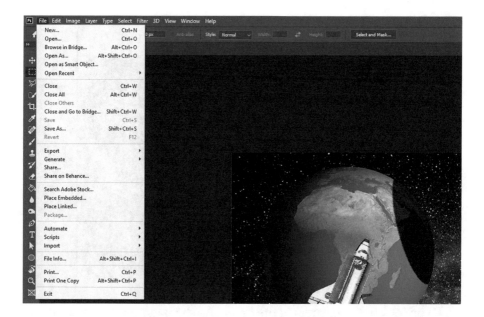

On the top right under "Printer Setup" select the printer, number of copies, and layout orientation.

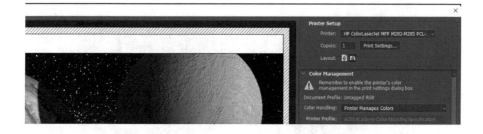

Using the print preview on the left you can adjust the image and fit it onto the page. Click and drag the image around.

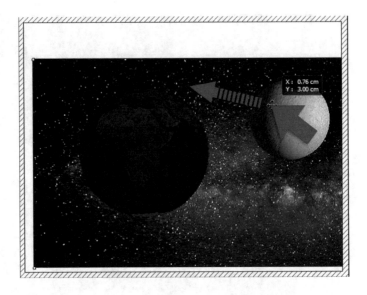

If you look at the corners of the image on the page, you'll see some resize handles. Click and drag these to resize the image.

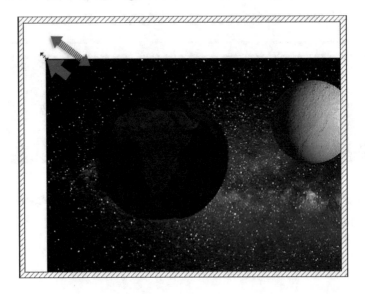

Using the position and scale section on the right, you can enter the sizes manually using the scale, height, and width. Or you can click "Scale to Fit Media" to automatically fit the image to the page.

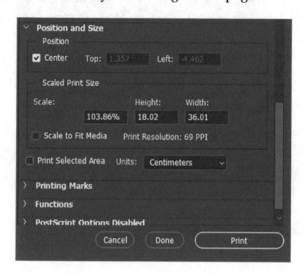

Click print when you're done.

Printing Part of an Image

Click on the Rectangle Marquee tool, then select the part of the image you want to print.

Go up to the file menu, select print.

From the print dialog box, scroll down the right-hand side, then tick Print Selected Area.

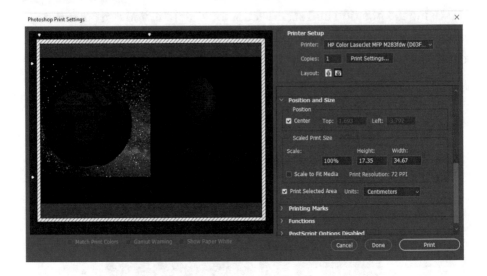

Click "Print" when you're done.

Lab Exercises

1. Find a photograph of your choice.

2. Open the photo in Photoshop.

3. Resize the image to a width of 1000 pixels.

4. Crop any areas of the image you want.

5. Adjust the hue and saturation.

6. Make the image brighter or darker.

7. Brighten any shadows and darken the highlights.

8. Add some text to the image.

9. Open another photo then flip it horizontally and
    rotate the image 90 degrees.

Summary

- You can import images from a scanner or camera.

- You can open a variety of different image formats in Photoshop.

- You can resize images (image ➤ resize).

- Rotate images (image ➤ image rotation).

- You can crop an image (use crop tool).

- Adjust lighting levels (image ➤ adjustments ➤ levels).

- Adjust brightness and contrast (image ➤ adjustments ➤ brightness/contrast).

- Transform and resize image (use marquee tool, right click, select free transform).

CHAPTER 4

Retouching Images

Photoshop can be used to touch up, enhance, and edit photographs and images; whether these are taken with a camera or created within Photoshop.

Photoshop has a vast array of tools and filters for you to use. In this chapter, we'll take a look at some of the most common tools and filters you can apply to your work.

For the demonstrations in this chapter, you'll need to download the resource files from the Photoshop section at

`github.com/apress/introduction-to-photoshop`

and extract them to your pictures folder, if you haven't already done so from previous chapters.

Burn Tool

The burn is used to darken an area. Open **house.png.**

In this example, we want to darken the trees behind the cabin.

Click and hold the cursor on the dodge tool in the toolbox. From the sub menu, select the burn tool.

Images are divided into highlights, the bright parts of the image (e.g., the sky), shadows (the darker parts), and midtones (everything in between). Since the part of the image, we want to darken is a midtone/shadow, make sure you select "Midtones" from the range on the options bar at the top. If the section is too dark, try "Shadows."

Select the size of the burn tool. The trees in the photo cover quite a large area, so a larger brush size would be better. Adjust the size slider and the hardness of the brush.

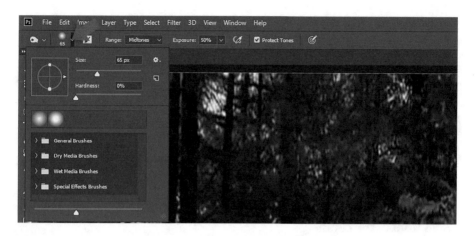

In the **house.png** image, use the burn tool to darken the trees in the background to make the cabin stand out more. Are these dark areas shadows or midtones? Try either of those settings and see what it does to the trees.

Notice how the midtones have been darkened, while the highlights haven't been touched.

If you wanted to darken the bright parts of the image, then select "Highlights" instead of "Midtones" from the "Range" drop-down box on the toolbar.

Dodge Tool

The dodge tool works in the opposite way to the burn tool and can be used to lighten a dark area of a picture to bring out the detail.

Open the **house.png** image and use the dodge tool to lighten the path just in front of the cabin.

Images are divided into highlights, the bright parts of the image, midtones, and shadows. Since the part of the image we want to lighten is a midtone/shadow, make sure you select "Midtones" from the range on the options bar at the top. If the section is too dark, try "Shadows."

Now click and drag the tool over the part of the image to lighten.

Spot Healing Tool

Open the **brightonlight.jpg** image. Select the spot healing brush tool from your tool box.

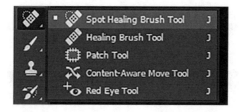

In this example, I'm going to use the spot healing tool to remove the sign post on the left-hand side of the image. Click the brush size on the bar at the top of the screen.

Adjust the size of the brush using the size slider to roughly the size of the sign we want to remove. Reduce the hardness of the brush to about 90%.

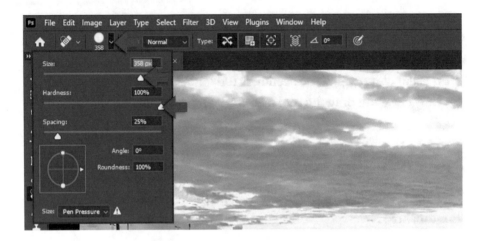

Along the top bar you'll see "Type." This is the type of repair you want to perform.

We'll use "Content Aware" for this example. You can see the difference demonstrated in the following.

Content   Create   Proximity
Aware   Texture   Match

"Content Aware" analyzes the surrounding area and attempts to interpret different parts of the image and generates a repair based on its analysis. This one usually produces the best results.

"Create Texture" generates a texture based on the surrounding area and fills in the area to be repaired.

"Proximity Match" samples the area surrounding the area to be repaired then generates a repair based on the data.

Now to repair the area, paint over the sign post as shown in the following.

When you release your mouse button, the area will be repaired.

Try experimenting with the three different types of the spot healing tool on different parts of the image. Try with content aware, create texture, and proximity match. See what happens.

Healing Brush Tool

Another useful tool is the heal tool. This tool uses samples in the surrounding area to replace the masked area of the image you selected.

In this example I'm going to use an old photograph that has been damaged.

Open oldimage.jpg

Select the healing brush tool from the tool box.

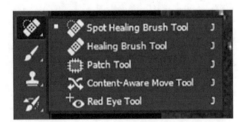

Alt-click (or option-click on a Mac) on an area that is clean and free of any damaged parts that are a similar brightness and color. This will be used as a "donor" to "heal" another area.

Now click the area to be repaired. Best to sample as near to the damaged area as possible.

Continue clicking on areas to be repaired, selecting new "donor" areas as the content of the image changes.

Patch Tool

The Patch tool is used to repair larger areas of an image to get rid of any distractions or blemishes.

Open **soccer.jpg**

Select the Patch tool from the toolbox on the left-hand side of the screen.

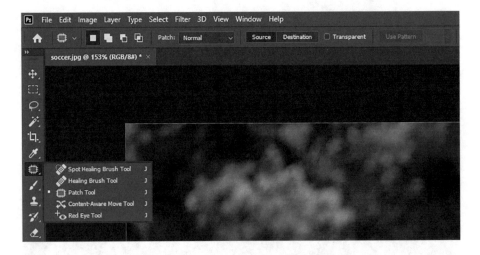

Draw around the object to select the area you want to remove. In this example, I want to remove the ball.

Click and drag the selection across to a nearby area that is clear and closely matches the surrounding area of the bit of the image you want to remove.

Once you release your mouse button, the area where the ball was will be patched with the area you sampled.

Content Aware Move Tool

Open the **brightonlight.jpg** image. In this image, say we wanted to move the bus a bit closer and a bit bigger in the image. First, select the content aware move tool from the healing brush section on your toolbox.

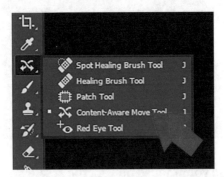

From the bar along the top of your screen set the "Mode" to "Move."

"Move mode" cuts out your selection and fills in the original position. "Extend mode" duplicates the selection.

Next trace around the bus in the image, as shown in the following.

Drag your selection toward the left as shown in the following. You can resize the selection using the resize handles on the surrounding box.

You can see Photoshop has attempted to remove the bus from its original position and has blended it into its new position.

The move isn't always 100% depending on the complexity and quality of your original image, so you may need to use the spot healing tool or the clone tool to touch up and repair the area.

Clone Stamp Tool

Sometimes it is necessary to remove an object from a photograph. We can do this with the Clone Stamp tool.

Open the **brightonlight.jpg** image.

In this photo, I want to get rid of the street sign in the image. It just ruins the shot. To do this use the clone stamp.

Change the size of your brush in the options bar until it's about the size of the following sign. Also select the hardness – set it to about 90%.

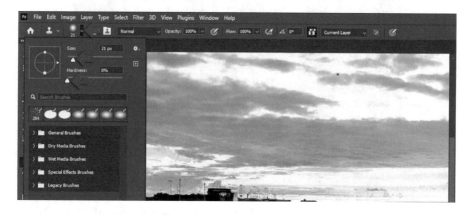

On your keyboard hold down Alt (or Option if you're on a Mac), then click an area close to the sign. This is the area we want to clone.

Try to sample as close to the spot you are going to remove as possible.

Paint over the sign a click at a time until the sign disappears.

Be patient and do it one click at a time as shown in the following. You'll notice as you move down the pole, the selected area moves parallel with it.

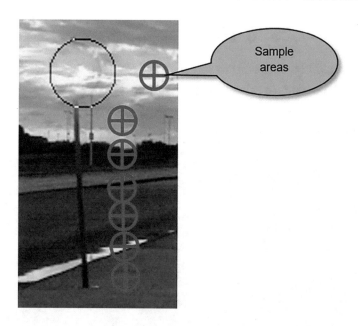

Challenge: Do the same with the sign's pole, this is a bit trickier as you have to clone the intricate details of the road.

Use the same technique as in the preceding to do a small edge next to the pole and clone.

Magnetic Lasso Tool

This tool is useful if you want to select an object in an image and not the background. We can do this with the magnetic lasso.

Open the **daffodils.jpg** image.

Use the magnetic lasso to select the daffodils in the photo.

Now trace around the daffodils with the lasso, you will find that it will magnetically stick to the edge of the yellow flower. Or press delete to move back a step.

You can now copy and paste this. Go to edit menu ➤ copy, then edit menu ➤ paste.

Quick Selection Tool

Sometimes it is necessary to remove an object from an image. This is useful if you want the object and not the background.

Open the **daffodils.jpg** image.

We can do this with the quick selection tool.

Use the quick selection tool to select the daffodils in the photo by clicking and dragging your mouse over the daffodils in the photo. Doing this increases that selection area.

To remove any selected area that you don't want, hold down alt/option and click that area to remove it from the selection

124

Magic Wand

The magic wand tool selects areas of similar tone and color.

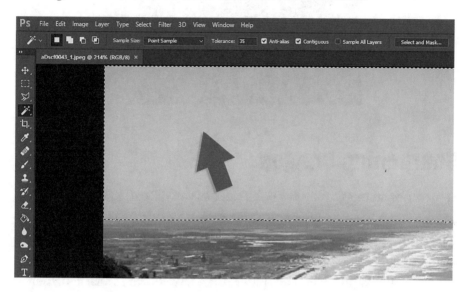

You can change the tolerance level in the options bar. The tolerance level is the difference in tone and color a pixel is from the next.

For example, if the tolerance level is set to 35, the magic wand will select any pixels that are the same color as the color you clicked on, plus any pixels up to 35 shades darker and 35 shades brighter.

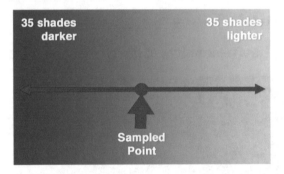

Sharpening Images

Sometimes an image may not be as clear as you'd like it to be. You can use the smart sharpen filter to try and clean up the image and make it a bit clearer. However, adding too much sharpness will make an image look worse, or it can lead to a loss in image detail.

Open molly.jpg. Select the "Filter" menu. Go down to sharpen, then select smart sharpen from the slideout menu.

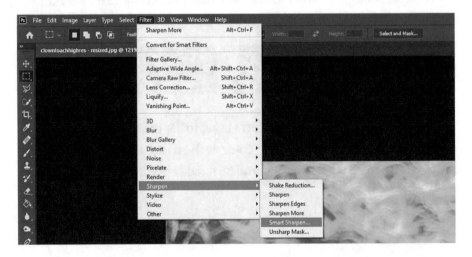

In the dialog box that opens, you'll see some options. At the top, you can select the amount of blur you want to remove. The radius is the size of the sharpening area around the edges in the image. For example, the value of 2 means sharpening over 2 pixels around the edge.

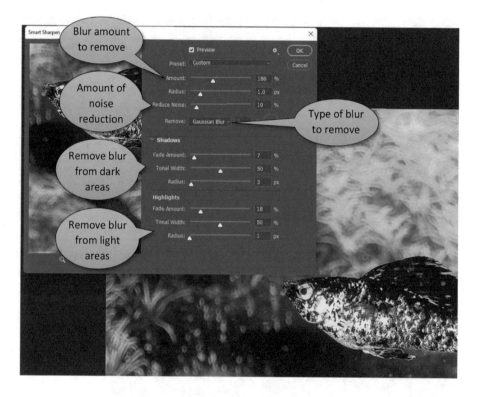

Move some of the sliders and see how it affects the image.

Camera RAW

Camera RAW is your digital darkroom where you can adjust a photograph's exposure, brightness, adjust highlights or shadows, correct white balance, remove digital noise, as well as straighten up photographs, remove lens distortion, and crop bits out.

Camera RAW automatically opens up when you open up a RAW image taken with your camera.

You can also find the Camera RAW filter on the filter menu in Photoshop.

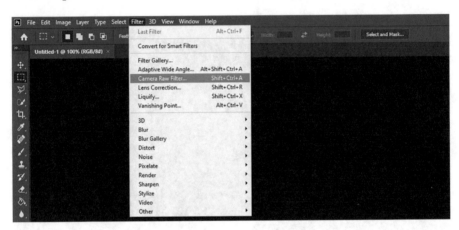

Let's take a look at the Camera RAW window. Here, you'll see a list of folders down the right-hand side. If you open one of the folders, for example "Basic," you'll see some settings appear.

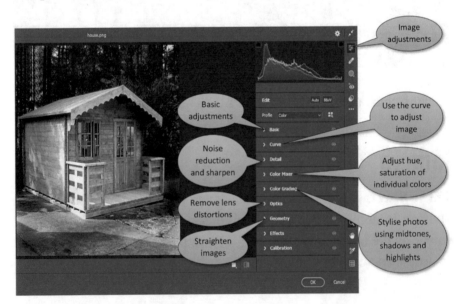

Using the basic settings, we can adjust the image using the sliders. You can change the exposure, temperature (blue or orange), highlights, and so on.

Reading a Histogram

On the top right of the camera raw window, you'll see a histogram. The histogram shows the tonal range of a photograph - the range of brightness levels from pure black to pure white in the photo.

If all your peaks are squashed over to the left, the photograph is under exposed or too dark.

If all the peaks are squashed over to the right, your photo is overexposed or too bright.

This isn't always the case and depends on the photograph. For example, if a photograph has a lot of dark areas and shadows, then the histogram peaks will be more over to the left.

Let's take a closer look at the histogram. The histogram is split into five sections: Blacks, Shadows, Midtones, Highlights, and Whites.

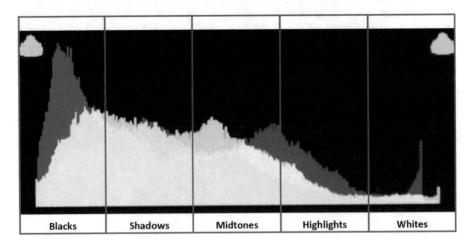

On a good histogram, most tones fall in the middle portion of the graph (shadows, midtones, and highlights) with little or nothing at the extreme edges.

Also on the histogram, you'll notice some color. Photoshop histograms show the brightness levels for all the primary colors: red, green, and blue channels (it also shows primary colors for print: yellow, cyan, and magenta).

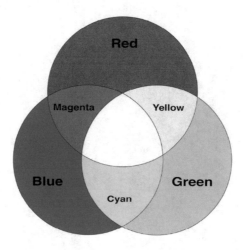

The light grey peak is the overall brightness. Don't worry too much about this now; for the scope of this exercise, concentrate on getting the peaks distributed across the five sections to achieve good exposure.

Basic Adjustments to a Photo

Open up **cameraraw.cr2** and have a go at adjusting the blacks, shadows, midtones, highlights, and whites using the camera raw filter, until you get a nice evenly spread histogram.

After you open the camera raw filter, select the "Adjustments" icon on the top right, then open the "Basic" folder on the right-hand side.

Keep an eye on the photograph to make sure it looks evenly exposed. This photo was shot with a canon camera in raw format.

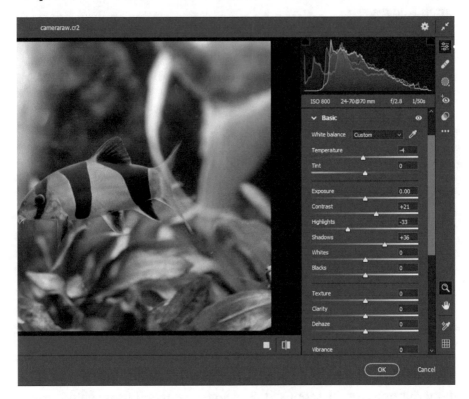

To adjust the photo, use the highlights, shadows, whites, and blacks sliders to adjust the relevant levels on the histogram. Use the exposure slider to adjust the overall brightness.

Using the Curve

Try the camera raw filter on **brighton.jpg.** Click the curve folder on the right-hand side. This is called the tone curve.

Select parabolic curve next to the "Adjust" section.

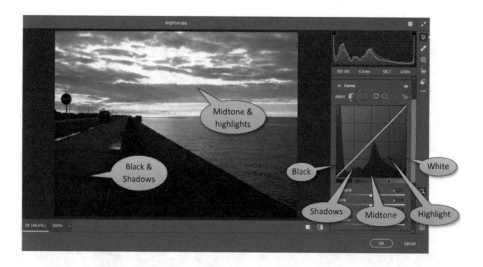

In this example, I'm going to increase the shadows on the road on the bottom left of the image. This part of the image is represented by the two sections on the left of the histogram.

Click on a point then drag it up. Try adjusting a few points on the curve and see what happens to the photo.

To further fine tune the image, select the "Point Curve" icon on the "Adjust" bar.

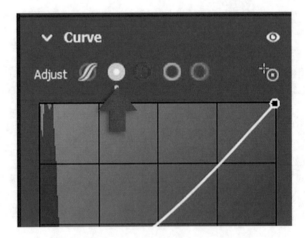

Now you can add points to the curve where you want to make adjustments. In our image brighton.jpg, we want to increase the shadows along the road.

This is indicated by the left part of the histogram.

To make adjustments, click the line to add a point.

In this example, I'm going to add a point to the shadows and bring up the brightness.

You'll notice that the shadows increase but also the brightness in the sky increases. To compensate for this, we need to add another point to bring down the sky. If you look at the histogram, you'll see a spike in the midtone section. This is the bit that represents the sky. We want to add a point here to bring this brightness down.

You can also adjust the primary colors separately. If you wanted to change just the reds, select red in the adjust bar. You can do the same for green and blue.

Click "OK" when you're done.

Noise Reduction and Sharpening

Try adding some noise reduction. To do so, open the detail folder on the right-hand side. Add some sharpening using the slider, then add some noise reduction. This helps to clean up the image.

Keep in mind that the "look" of the photograph will depend on the monitor you are using and whether it is correctly set up or calibrated. For example, if your brightness is turned up quite high on your monitor, your photo will look brighter than it actually is.

Leveling Photos and Removing Lens Distortion

When taking photographs, depending on what lens you use, there is always some kind of distortion. One of the most common issues seen when taking photographs of buildings and architecture, is the angle of walls.

Open **cathedral.jpg** and have a look.

Because the photographer has had to angle the camera upwards to get the whole tower in, the walls are all slanted inwards. Not a very professional looking photo.

You can use the camera raw filter to remove this distortion. Select the geometry folder from the tool bar at the top of the camera raw window.

On the right-hand side, under the histogram, you'll see some adjustment controls. First, try the auto adjustments, sometimes these do a good enough job. I'm going to try auto first. Click the "A" icon.

It did an OK job, but didn't remove the distortion completely. To fine tune the adjustments, open "Manual Transformations."

The vertical and horizontal controls work well with slanting walls. You will probably also need to enlarge the scale, using the scale slider, as the photo will warp a little bit when applying the corrections. Try them out, see what each slider does.

Click OK on the bottom right when you're happy.

Looks a lot better right? You might lose some of the image, but it's a small price to pay for a better-looking photograph.

Lab Exercises

1. Find an image of your choice and open it in
    Photoshop.

2. Use the burn tool to darken some parts of the image.

3. Use the dodge tool to brighten some parts of
    the image.

4. Find an old image with spots, tears, and blemishes.

5. Use the spot healing tool and clone tools to clean up
    the image and remove the blemishes.

6. Open up an image in Photoshop, then use the
    camera raw filter to make some adjustments.
    Experiment with the various options to see what
    they do.

Summary

- The burn is used to darken an area.

- The dodge tool is used to lighten a dark area of a
  picture to bring out the detail.

- The heal tool uses samples in the surrounding area to
  replace the selected area of the image you selected.

- Clone Stamp tool allows you to sample a part of
  the image and use it to paint over another part of
  the image.

- The magnetic lasso selects an object in an image and
  not the background when you trace around it.

- Quick selection tool allows you to select a portion of the image.

- The magic wand tool selects areas of similar tone and color.

- Camera RAW is your digital darkroom where you can adjust a photograph's exposure, brightness, adjust highlights or shadows, correct white balance, remove digital noise, as well as straighten up photographs, remove lens distortion, and crop bits out.

- The histogram shows the tonal range of a photograph - the range of brightness levels from pure black to pure white in the photo.

CHAPTER 5

Layers

A layer is a transparent canvas where you can add text, images, and other graphics independently. Layers are piled on top of each other in a stack to form the complete image or design.

You can think of a layer as a transparent sheet of glass or acetate stacked on top of another. You can see the sheets underneath through any transparent areas of the top sheet. Each layer contains its own graphics, text, or photographs depending on what the image is.

Photoshop allows you to build up complex designs using multiple layers to contain elements or objects that make up parts of the whole design - like building blocks. This means that each element in the design can be created, edited, and moved around independently without affecting everything else. These elements could be a text, photographs, illustrations, shapes, and so on. This is where Photoshop really shows its power.

For the demonstrations in this chapter, you'll need to download the resource files from the Photoshop section at

github.com/apress/introduction-to-photoshop

and extract them to your pictures folder, if you haven't already done so from previous chapters.

Let's begin by taking a look at a simple example.

© Kevin Wilson 2023
K. Wilson, *Introduction to Photoshop*, https://doi.org/10.1007/978-1-4842-8963-1_5

The Layers Concept

As we mentioned earlier, layers are like transparent sheets of glass stacked on top of each other. We add layers to contain our effects, images, and Photoshop objects. This means we can edit, resize, and position them in place without affecting the other layers. In the following example, I have a text layer for the title "planet Earth" (layer 2), and a photograph on another layer underneath.

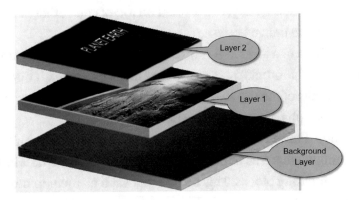

Figure 5-1. *Layers of an Image*

The background layer is a special type that serves primarily as a background. This layer is usually locked, meaning you can't move it, add any effects, or change the opacity. When you open a PNG or JPEG image, or a new Photoshop project, it opens as a background layer in the layers panel as we can see in the following. Here I've opened a Photoshop project that is 600 x 600px in size with a black background.

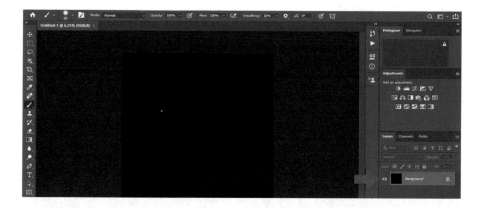

You build up your project by adding additional layers on top of the background layer as we can see in Figure 5-1. Let's add the earth image (earth.png). This image has the planet earth on the bottom left with the rest of the image transparent.

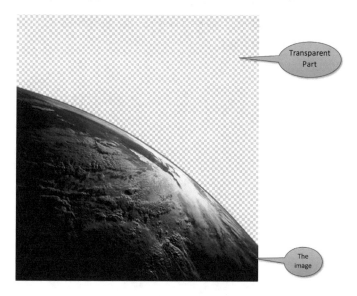

Navigate to the image using File Explorer in Windows (or Finder if you're using a Mac). Drag and drop the picture onto the Photoshop project we opened earlier.

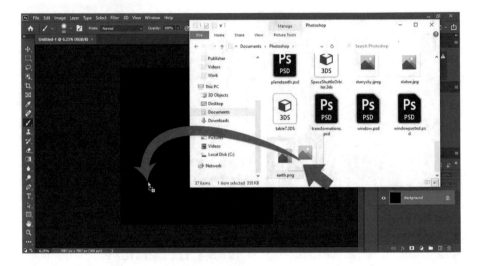

Once the image appears on your project, you might need to resize it to fill the canvas. Notice on the layers panel that the earth.png image has been added as another layer. You can see the background through the transparent part of the image.

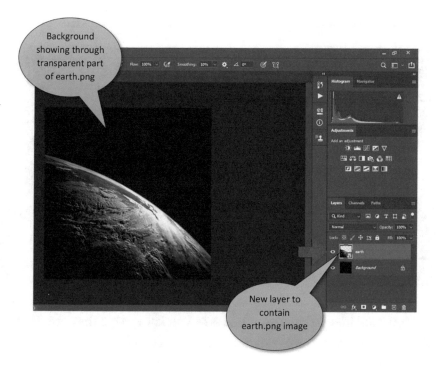

Let's add a title. Select the text tool then draw a textbox in the black part of the image. Type in "Planet Earth." We'll change the text to white and make it larger.

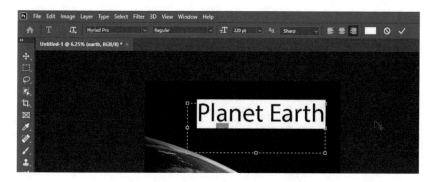

Move it into position on the top right of the canvas. Click the tick icon on the top right of the options bar.

Notice that Photoshop has added a new layer to contain the text.

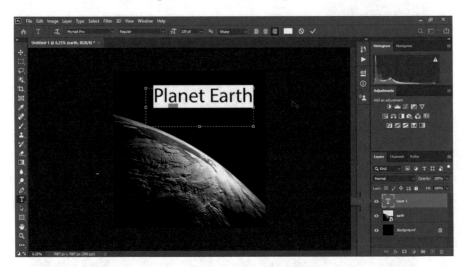

It's a good idea to label your layers so you know what they are. To do this, double-click the layer's name in the panel ("Layer 1"), then type in a meaningful name. Note that text layers will often become the name of the text after you click the check in the options bar. In Figure 5-2, we can see the Photoshop layers below in the layers panel.

Figure 5-2. *Photoshop Layers*

What's the point of all these layers, you might ask. Why can't I just dump all my objects and text on the page?

Well you could, but if you did that, it would be a nightmare to design, edit, and change later on. What if you put the text in the wrong place or wanted to change font? Or change or move an image you inserted? Once you save the image, all the text, graphics and photos are flattened (or merged) so you can't change them easily.

The idea behind using layers is that you can independently arrange the objects out on the canvas to create your design. You can move them around, try objects or text in different places to see what looks good. You can add effects to individual objects without affecting the others, you can also change an image or text later if you need to. In this way, you can build up multilayered projects and designs piece by piece and save them as multilayered projects (PSD files) instead of flat images (PNG or JPEG files).

For example, carrying on with our little project, we can add some blending effects to the layers. We could add an outer glow to the text.

To do this, double-click the text layer in the layers panel on the bottom right-hand side of your screen to open the layer style dialog box. Make sure you click the actual layer not the text.

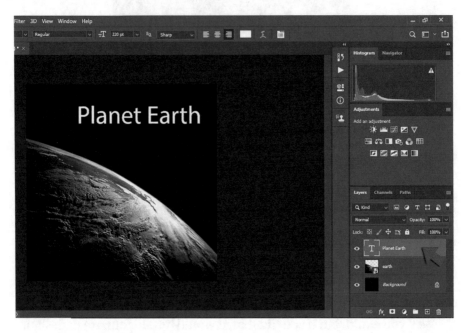

Click on outer glow, on the left-hand side. In the outer glow settings, change the color to yellow, then experiment with the opacity, spread, and size effects and see what happens.

Notice that the effect is applied only to the text layer and not to the earth image layer. The effect appears in an "Effects" section (fx) on the layer in the layers panel on the right.

You can double-click this if you need to change it later. Or you can click the "Eye" icon to hide/show the effect.

Try some of the other effects and see what happens.

Now that we understand layers a little better, let's take a look at what you can do...

Create an Image Collage

A collage is made up of two or more separate images. We'll use two images in this example; you can add more if you wish.

Open the **house.png** image. Using the magnetic lasso tool, make a selection around the cabin. If you are having trouble keeping the line on the edge of the cabin, try increasing the contrast or the frequency in the options bar.

Trace all the way around the edge of the cabin. When you close the loop, you will see the "marching ants" around marking your selection.

Right click your mouse on the "marching ants" selection, and from the popup menu select "feather." Set it to about 2px. This just softens the edge of the selected image.

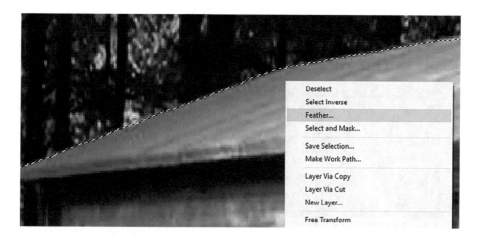

Go to edit menu, select copy.

Now load up **lake.psd** then go to edit menu and select paste. The cabin will appear on a new layer titled "Layer 1," in the layers panel.

With Layer 1 still highlighted in the layers panel, go to the edit menu, go down to transform then select scale. Drag the resize handles inwards as shown in the following.

Reduce the image to about 1/3 of its original size or until it fits nicely. Double-click the selection to execute the transform.

Using the move tool, place this image on the grass bank next to the water, so it looks like it's next to the river.

A challenge for you. Notice the edges along the bottom of the cabin don't quite look like they're sitting on the grass. See if you can remove these and make it look a bit more realistic. Try a few different tools such as the eraser. Perhaps try the clone tool.

Selection and Free Transform

Using the transform and scale tools, it is possible to resize and move objects, shapes, or images on a particular layer.

Open the file **moon.png.**

Using the marquee tool select the moon.

Copy this selection. Go to the edit menu, select copy.

Open up the **planetearth.psd** file.

Go to edit menu, select paste. You may need to use the free transform tool to resize the moon image.

Make sure the image you just pasted is behind the earth.

To put the moon behind the earth, go over to your layers panel and drag "Layer 1" below the "Earth" layer.

Make sure "Layer 1" is selected in the layers panel.

Go to edit menu, go down to transform, then select scale.

Drag the handles, circled as follows, so that the moon seems smaller than the earth. When you're satisfied, double-click the moon image to execute the scale.

Layer Effects

Carrying on from the last section, if not, open the file **planetearth.psd**

Double-click the earth layer in the layers panel to bring up layer style dialog box.

Click "Outer Glow." Change the spread to a value of 26% and the size to a value of 100 px.

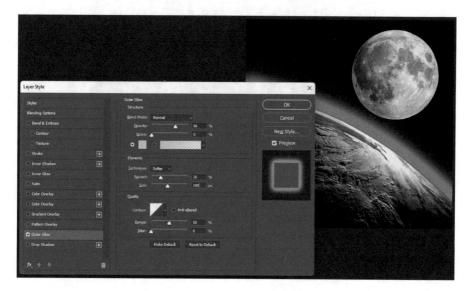

Click "OK" when you're done.

Add Text

Let's use some text to title our image. Photoshop uses vector mapping to create text - so you can scale the text to any size without pixelation.

Carrying on from the last section, if not, open **planetearth.psd**

Select the horizontal text tool from your toolbox. Select a nice font (e.g., myriad pro), size (e.g., 61pt) and color (e.g., #3d81ff) in the options bar shown in the following.

Click and drag the text box across the moon on the image where you want to place the text.

Type in a title. My title in this example is "Planet Earth."

Double-click the text layer you just created in the layers panel to bring up the layer style dialog box.

Select "Bevel and Emboss" from the list on the left hand side.

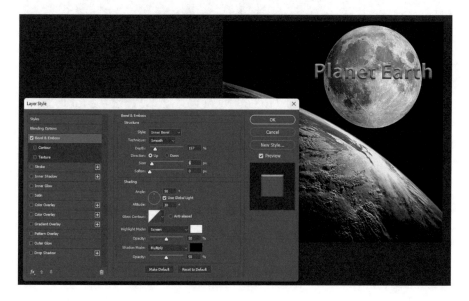

Using the "Structure" and "Shading Settings," try a different style: "inner bevel," or "outer bevel." Try changing the size and depth of the bevel. Also see what happens when you change the shading angles.

Try experimenting with different styles to see what effects you can add. How about a nice outer glow?

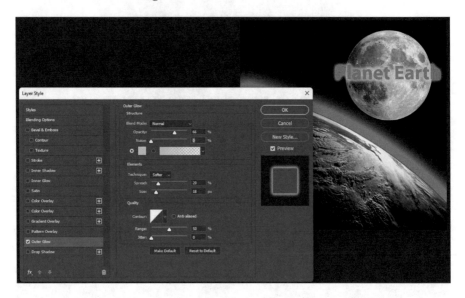

Adjust the opacity, try changing the spread or size. Click "OK" when you're done.

Now we can move this text to wherever we want. From the toolbox, select the Move Tool. To adjust the position of this text, place the Move Tool on your text, click and drag it to the correct location.

Smart Objects

When you drag and drop a photograph or object into a Photoshop image, the object is pasted as a new layer and adopts the characteristics of the Photoshop image.

If you paste it in as a smart object, you can edit and build the object as an independent image with its own characteristics, layers, effects, and so on. A smart object could be another Photoshop (PSD) image or a design from Illustrator.

To embed a Photoshop image or Illustrator design, select the file menu then click "Place Embedded."

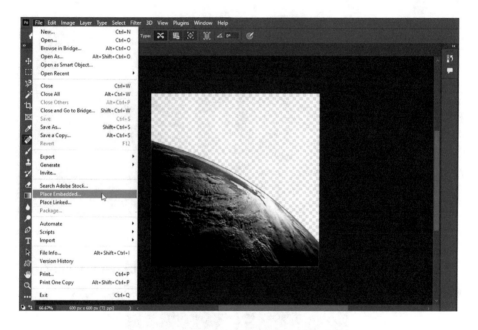

Navigate to and select the file you want to add.

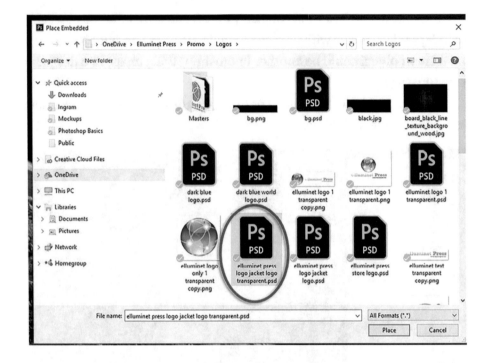

Click "Place."

On your layers panel you'll see a small logo on the bottom right of the layer thumbnail. This means that the layer contains a smart object.

Now you can directly edit the smart object. To do this, double-click the layer thumbnail on your layers panel.

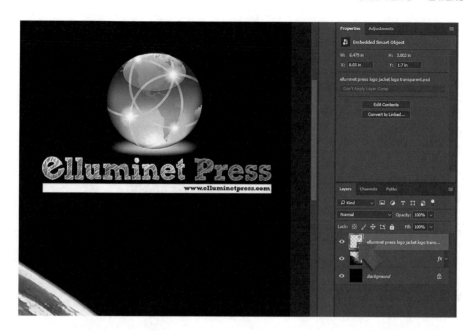

The smart object will open up in a new Photoshop window.

The layers panel will change to show the layers of the smart object you just opened. Here you can make independent changes and edit the object.

Once you are done, save and close the object file (file ➤ save) and it will automatically update.

Adjustment Layers

Adjustment layers alter all the layers below them, which makes them ideal for adjusting color, contrast, brightness without altering individual layers.

You can find your basic adjustments on the adjustment panel. If the panel isn't open, go to the window menu and select "Adjustments."

The adjustments available are shown in the following.

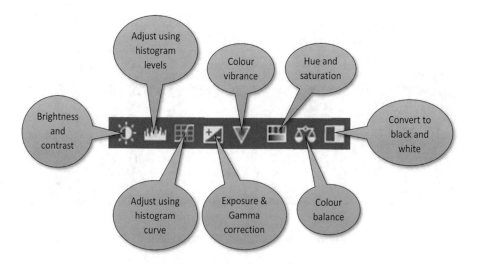

A few more advanced adjustments you can perform.

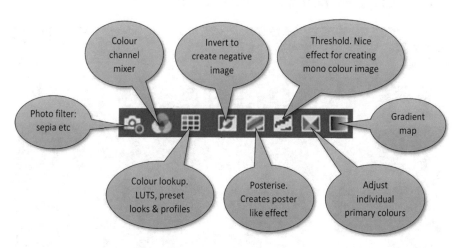

To apply any of these adjustments, click the icon.

For this example, open **windowpasted.psd**. Notice that this project has multiple layers. Say I wanted to adjust the whole brightness or contrast of the whole image. If I attempt to use the adjustments on the image menu, the adjustment is only applied to the selected layer.

To apply an adjustment layer, select the top layer of your project (layer 2). Remember the adjustment layer affects all layers underneath it.

From the adjustment panel, select the "Brightness" icon. Notice an adjustment layer has been added in the layers panel

Some controls will appear in the properties panel. For this particular adjustment layer, we have brightness and contrast sliders. Move these until you have the desired brightness. Try applying some of the other adjustment layers see what they do.

Auto-align Layers

This is a great feature if you have multiple shots of the same scene you want to blend together.

A common example is a group shot at a wedding where not everyone is looking at the camera, some have their eyes closed because they blinked or looked away. If you have a number of different shots taken one after the other, you can combine the best ones to create a new image. This only works with images that have similar contents.

For this to work, your images need to be taken from the same perspective - the same position. Photoshop can't align the images if they're very different or taken from different angles. Try it, see what happens.

Let's take a look at a simple example. Go to your file menu and select open.

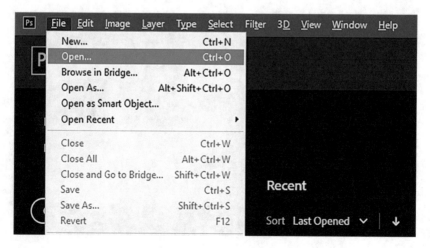

Open the file **one.jpg** from the auto align folder in the accompanying resources.

Open your file explorer or finder and navigate to the auto align folder, then drag and drop **two.jpg** on top of the open image. The image you just imported will be added as another layer.

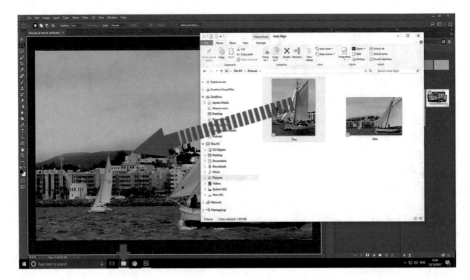

Notice how the layers don't match and it would make a nice image if these two shots were combined.

To auto align the layers, first make sure all your layers are rasterized. If not, right click the layer name in the layers panel and select "rasterize layer" from the popup menu.

Next select both layers. Hold down control or command and click each layer.

From the edit menu, select "Auto-Align Layers."

Select "Auto" from the dialog box, then click "OK."

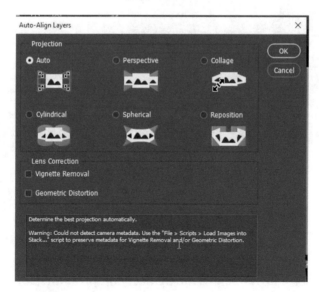

Photoshop will analyze the layers and attempt to align them together.

You might need to crop the image to remove any edges.

You can see it has created a much nicer composition than the original.

Layer Opacity and Fill

The opacity of a layer determines how transparent or opaque the layer is. In other words, it controls how much the layers below show through. Open **opacityfill.psd**.

Fill will change the transparency of whatever is filling the layer, but will ignore any effects or blend modes that have been applied.

To change the opacity, select the desired layer, then click the opacity drop-down arrow at the top of the Layers panel.

Click and drag the slider to adjust the opacity. You'll see the layer opacity change in the document window as you move the slider.

If you set the opacity to 0%, the layer will become completely transparent, or invisible.

If you want to change the fill opacity, click the fill drop-down box instead. Fill Opacity is used when you don't want the Opacity of the effect to disappear as well.

Blending Modes

Blend modes are used to determine how layers are blended with each other. There are various different categories of blend modes. Let's take a look at what they are.

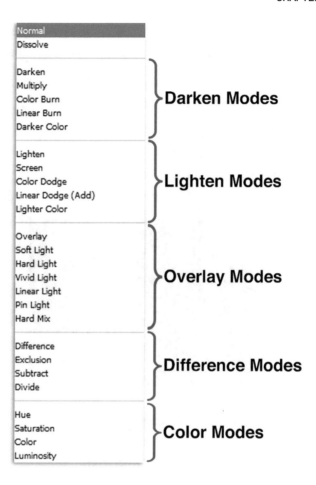

- Normal Blending shows your layer as it currently is.

- Darken Modes darken the dark pixels and makes white pixels transparent.

- Lighten Modes lighten dark pixels while making blacks transparent.

- Overlay Modes make all pixels that are 50% grey become transparent while lighter pixels get lighter and darker pixels get darker.

- Difference Modes make the pixels in the blend layer and layer underneath become opposite of each other.

- Color Modes use hue (color), saturation (intensity of color), and luminosity (brightness) to create the blending effects.

Open the file **blendmodes.psd**.

In the layers panel, you'll see two layers. Select the shuttle layer. This is the layer we want to blend into the layer underneath (Color Fill 1).

You'll see a whole list of blend modes appear.

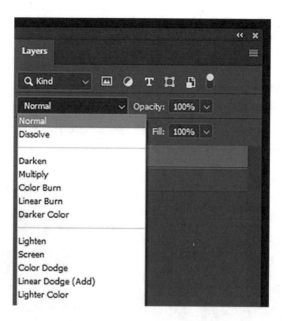

Run through the list and see what each of the blend modes do and note how it affects the shuttle image.

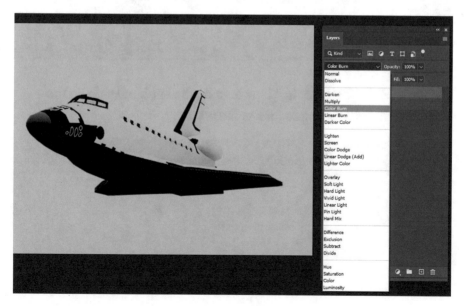

You can save your file once you're done.

Lab Exercise

In this exercise, we're going to build a slide using various different effects, images, and layers.

Open the file **videoslide.psd**. This file contains a background image.

Insert **person.png** into the project. Make sure you resize and move the image so it fits nicely on the screen.

Now add some text in the blank area on the left-hand side. In the example, I'm creating a slide for a video course.

Select a font, color, and resize the text so it looks good. Add a shadow to the text to make it stand out a bit.

Decorate the rest of the slide with some different types of brushes, maybe a splash of paint.

Try out a few of the other effects.

Perhaps add a shape to fill the bottom left corner.

Or try and insert another image (e.g., use shuttle.png)

Try some blending modes on the text and the shuttle layers.

Summary

- A layer is a transparent canvas where you can add text, images, and other graphics independently. Layers are stacked on top of each other in a stack to form the complete image or design.

- Use the transform and scale tools to resize and move objects, shapes, or images on a particular layer.

- A smart object is an independent image with its own characteristics, layers, effects, etc.

- Adjustment layers allow you to add image adjustments to your photos. Adjustments could be brightness, contrast, hue, saturation filters. They are added as layers so you can change or remove the adjustments later. Or you can add the adjustments to multiple layers below the adjustment layer.

- Auto-align layer is a great feature if you have multiple shots of the same scene you want to blend together.

CHAPTER 6

Special Effects

Photoshop has a large number of filters that you can apply to your images and give them a special look or characteristic.

Filters range from those that apply a particular painting effect to those that imitate different camera settings.

For the demonstrations in this chapter, you'll need to download the resource files from the Photoshop section at

`github.com/apress/introduction-to-photoshop`

and extract them to your pictures folder, if you haven't already done so from previous chapters.

Filters

Photoshop has a large number of filters that allow you to add effects to your images.

- Sharpen filter (which helps sharpen up the edges of a slightly blurry image)

- Blur Effects (which can be used to create soft out-of-focus areas on an image)

- Lighting Effects

- Artistic Effects

You can find all your filters on the filters menu.

K. Wilson, *Introduction to Photoshop*, https://doi.org/10.1007/978-1-4842-8963-1_6

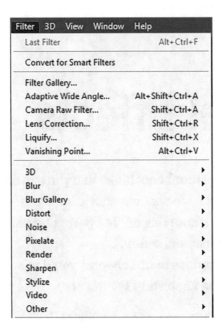

You can also browse through them in the filters gallery.

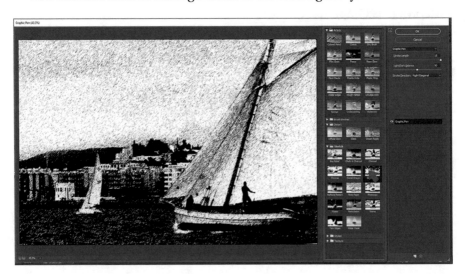

Here you can browse through the filters, circled in the preceding in red, and view the effects on your image.

Blur

Open the **car.jpg** image. From the filter menu, go down to "Blur," then select "Motion Blur." The entire image now looks like the car is moving really fast.

In the dialog box that appears, you can adjust the amount of blur, and the angle of blur.

Experiment with applying different amounts of blur using the slider at the bottom of the window. Try the two different methods angles to see what effect they have on the image.

Try some of the other blur options in the blur slideout such as gaussian, lens, and smart blur on the filters menu.

Stylize Filters

Stylize filters allow you to create a painted or impressionistic effect on your images. Select "Stylize" from the "Filter" menu.

From the slideout, select "Oil Paint." Turn your image into a Van Gogh. Click the check box next to "Preview," then use the sliders on the right-hand side of the dialog box for stylization and detail of the oil paint effect. Try each one and see what it does to the image.

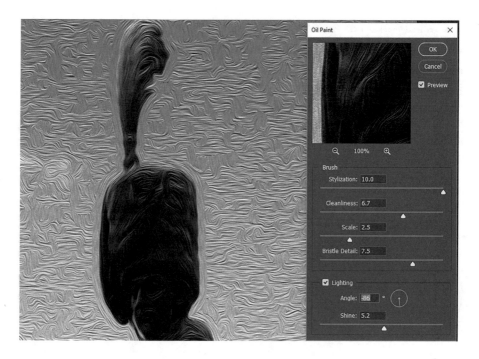

Filter Gallery

The filter gallery is useful for trying different filters and seeing the immediate result in the preview window. This helps you experiment and try out new ideas without applying the filter each time.

Open the file **statue.jpg** from the resources folder.

Open the filter gallery. Go to the filter menu and select "Filter Gallery."

When you open the filter gallery, you'll see a preview of the currently open image on the left and a list of filters and controls on the right-hand side.

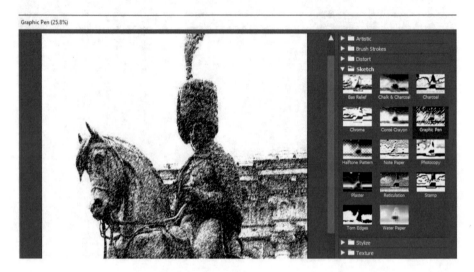

To apply the filters, open up the folders and select a thumbnail. In this example, I'm going to apply a graphic pen filter from the sketch folder to my image.

Now, over on the right hand side of the screen, you'll see some controls that allow you to adjust the effect of the filter. These tend to change depending on which filter you've selected. In this case, you can adjust the length of each pen stroke, the amount of light and dark strokes, and the direction of the pen stroke.

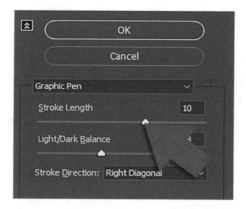

Try adjusting these using the sliders and see what happens to the image. Click "OK" when you're happy to apply the filter to the image. Here's an example.

Try some of the other filters and see what happens.

Lighting Effects

Lighting effects in Photoshop requires 3D functionality - so you will need a graphics card, and an OS that supports OpenGL and 3D functionality. It should be noted that there are some issues with this filter in the most recent versions of Photoshop and the application may stall when using this filter. Please refer to the following links for more information.

`helpx.adobe.com/photoshop/using/add-lighting-effects1.html`

and

`helpx.adobe.com/photoshop/kb/3d-faq.html`

To check, go to preferences, go up to the "Edit" menu, then select "Preferences." Select "Performance." If you're using a Mac, select the "Photoshop" menu.

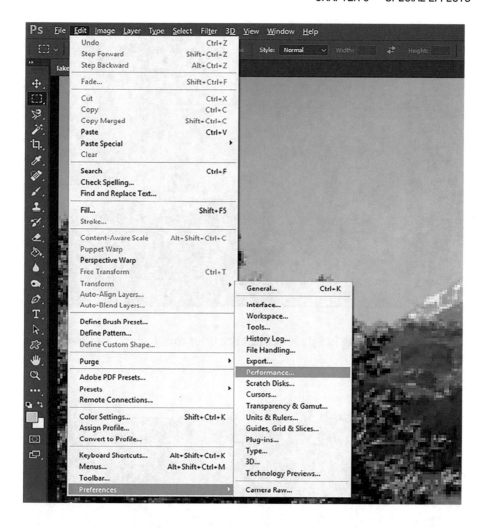

Is "Use Graphics Processor" checked, or is it greyed out? If its greyed out, you will have to use the classic effects.

Lighting effects only supports 8 bit/channel RGB images. Change this using the "Image" menu. Select the settings from the "Mode" slideout.

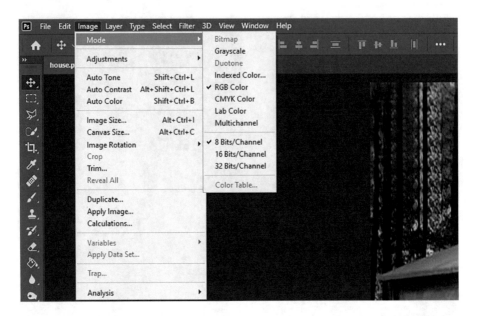

Open **house.png** image and from the filter menu click "Render" then "Lighting Effects."

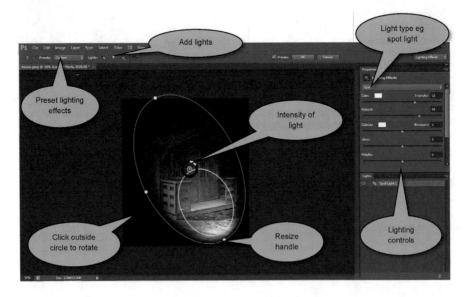

From the lighting effects panel on the right-hand side you can choose a number of different types of lights, color, and adjust the intensity, direction, and focus.

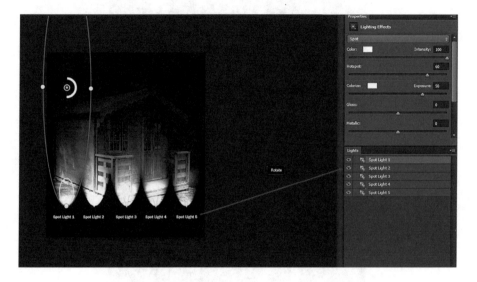

Drag the lights into position.

Drag the resize handles to resize and rotate the lights.

Try experimenting with different light settings.

Here I added two spot lights, changed the color and intensity, and arranged them outside my house.

Combining Photos

You can use the selection tools and the "Paste into" command to create interesting special effects.

In the following example, lightning will be added behind the windows in a second photo to give the effect that the there is a storm inside a building.

Open the **lightning.jpg** image.

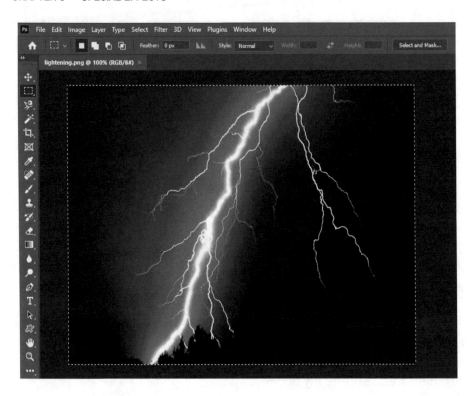

Select the rectangular marquee tool from the toolbox, then press control A (or command A if you're on a Mac) to select the whole image.

Use the copy command from the edit menu, to copy the selection to the clipboard.

Open the **window.psd** image.

Select the polygon marquee tool.

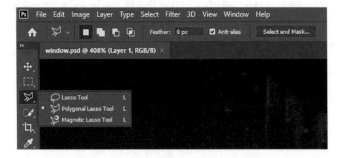

Start in one of the square window panes. You might want to zoom right into your picture to do this. Click in the top left corner inside the frame, line up the line marker that appears along the frame, click in the second corner.

Go around the pane, then click back on the point in the top left corner to complete the selection.

Hold down the shift key, then select the other full window panes in the same way until all the sky blue is selected, but not the window frames.

When you get to the top section where you don't have any straight lines, use the magnetic lasso tool and trace around the edges.

You could also try the magic wand tool to select this bit.

You'll end up with something like this in the following image. Note that only the blue sky is selected not the curtains or the window frames.

Once all the window panes are selected, go to the edit menu, select paste special. From the slideout select the "Paste into."

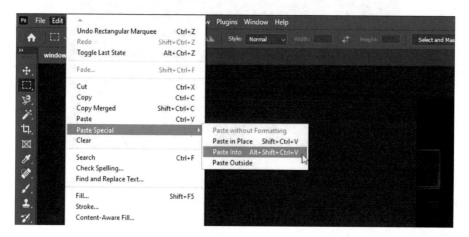

This will paste in lightning picture we copied earlier. The "paste into" command pastes the lightning picture we copied behind the window panes we cut out into a layer mask which we will look at next.

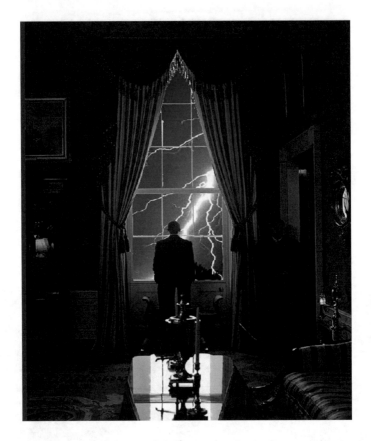

Now select the "Move Tool" from your toolbox, then move the lightning picture around until you like the effect in the windows.

The window picture has effectively become a mask for the lightning picture which lies behind it.

A challenge for you. You might have noticed that there is a reflection on the table.

See if you can create a reflection of the lightning storm on the table to match the one seen through the window. Consider what tools or commands from previous chapters could be used to accomplish this.

Layer Masks

Photoshop layer masks control the transparency of a layer. In other words, a layer mask conceals or shows different parts of an image. So, a layer mask can be used to hide a specific area, or to make other areas of a layer visible.

Open the file **masks.psd.** This file has a background image called lightning, and an image of a cathedral. I have set up the file this way so you can clearly see the effects of the layer mask.

Add a layer mask to the layer in the layers panel. To do this, click the layer you want to add a mask to, then click the layer mask button at the bottom of the layers panel.

A layer mask thumbnail will appear beside the image layer thumbnail in the layers panel.

When using layer masks, black areas of the mask become transparent, whereas white areas are opaque.

Select the brush tool, then make your foreground color black. In this example, I want to conceal the sky in the following image. Paint over any parts of the image you want to conceal with your brush.

You'll see these areas become transparent. You'll also see black appear in the mask on the layers panel

Because these areas have now become transparent, you'll see the image on the layer below show through.

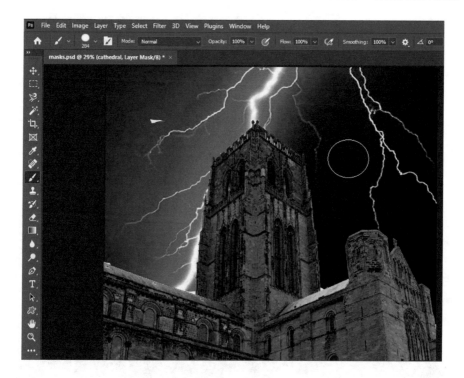

Select the brush tool and choose white as the foreground color. Paint any areas of the image you want to appear with the brush tool. When you first make the layer mask, the entire layer will default to white.

If you want to blend anything such as the edges, choose a shade of gray as the foreground color. The darker the gray, the more transparent the area of the image will be.

Paint over any part of a layer you want partially visible or faded.

Clipping Mask

A clipping mask connects multiple layers together and forms a shared mask based on the shape of the bottommost layer. The bottom layer will define where the clipped layers are visible, based on the shape or layer mask of that layer. Clipping masks are useful for applying adjustment onto a specific layer or to alter the shape of an image.

207

Open the file **clippingmask.psd**

Here in the example, we have two layers (not including the background).

The simplest way to create a clipping mask is to right-click a layer we want to mask, in this example the photo layer. From the popup menu, select "Create Clipping Mask."

This will clip the selected layer to the underlying layer in the Layers panel. In this case, the hexagon on the polygon layer. In the layers palette, on the photo layer we applied the clipping mask to, you'll notice a little down arrow to the left of the thumbnail. This indicates that this layer is clipped to the layer underneath.

If you need to release the clipping mask, right-click the clipped layer, then select "Release Clipping Mask."

Summary

- You can use filters to sharpen or blur an image. You'll find these on the filters menu.

- Add lighting effects (in the filters menu, go to render, select lighting effects)

- Paste an image into a selection (edit, paste special, paste into)

- Layer masks control the transparency of a layer. Black is transparent, white is opaque

- A clipping mask connects multiple layers together and forms a shared mask based on the shape of the bottommost layer.

CHAPTER 7

3D Effects

3D functionality requires a capable graphics card, and an OS that can support OpenGL, OpenCL, and 3D features.

A good Nvidia Quadro or GeForce graphics/video card is recommended for Adobe applications and will allow you to use all the advanced features in Photoshop.

Note that there are some issues with the functionality of 3D feature in the most recent versions and using these might cause Photoshop to stall or not act as expected. This might affect

- All interactions in the 3D workspace.

- 3D printing.

- Normal Map and Bump Map filters (including smart objects with those filters applied).

- Any/all extrusions, including text extrusions.

- Spherical Panorama editing and support.

- Import/Export of all 3D formats.

Please refer to the following Links and edit this section. And refer to technology preview note:

helpx.adobe.com/photoshop/using/add-lighting-effects1.html

or

helpx.adobe.com/photoshop/kb/3d-faq.html

© Kevin Wilson 2023
K. Wilson, *Introduction to Photoshop*, https://doi.org/10.1007/978-1-4842-8963-1_7

For the demonstrations in this chapter, you'll need to download the resource files from the Photoshop section at

`github.com/apress/introduction-to-photoshop`

and extract them to your pictures folder, if you haven't already done so from previous chapters.

Creating 3D Objects

For this exercise, open up **earthmap.jpg**

To start using 3D, you'll need to open up the 3D panel. Go to the window menu and select "3D." A panel will open on the right-hand side of your screen.

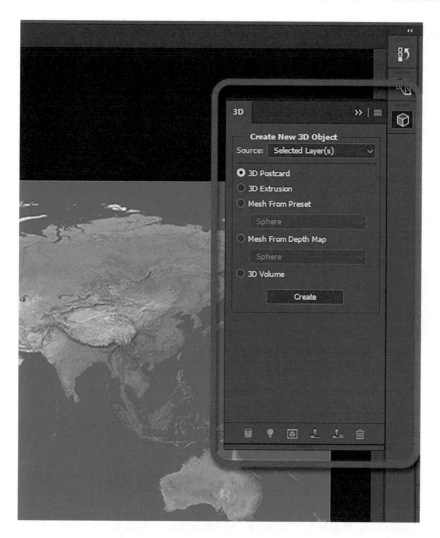

Here you'll be able to create 3D objects from layers, paths, or objects.

3D Postcard

The easiest way to create 3D is by taking a layer and generating a 3D plane, or postcard. With the background layer set as your source, choose 3D Postcard from the 3D tab and Photoshop will create a 3D plane based on the pixels in your layer.

A postcard is also useful if you want to generate a plane to catch reflections, shadows, lighting, effects, etc. You can orient the plane perpendicular to your object and then merge the 3D objects together to a single layer.

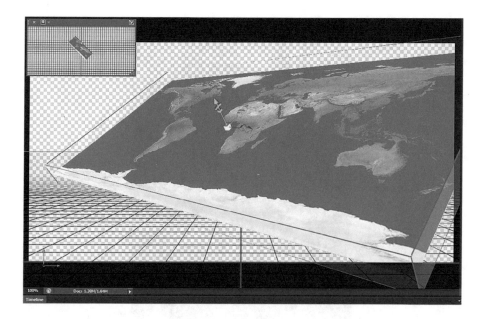

3D Extrusion

To create a 3D extrusion, select "Extrusion" from the 3D panel on the bottom right of your screen. Select 3D extrusion on the 3D tab on the layers panel.

Add some text with the text tool.

3D Shape from Preset

You can also take this layer and wrap it around any 3D shape, such as a sphere, cube, cylinder, and so on.

Open **earthmap.jpg**

In this example, I am going to take the map of the earth and wrap it around a sphere.

From the 3D panel, click "Mesh from Preset." Then change the shape selection to "Sphere."

Click "Create" at the bottom of the 3D panel when you've done that.

Add Some 3D Text

Select your text tool and type some text next to the 3D earth. Then hit your 3D button to convert it to a 3D object.

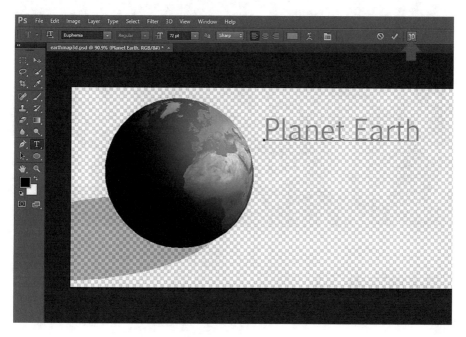

Click the text object and using the 3D controls position your text accordingly so it looks good next to the planet.

Navigating 3D

Let's take a brief look at the 3D controls for moving and sizing your 3D objects.

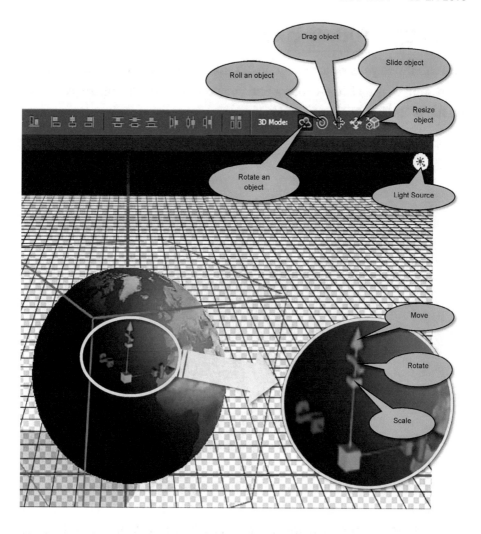

Each 3D object has a handle with three axes on it. These axes are for moving and manipulating the object in 3D space.

- Red is X-axis (left/right)

- Green is Y-axis (up/down)

- Blue is Z-axis (nearer/farther)

Moving Around Your Object

You can move your view around in 3D space. Your view point is usually represented by a virtual camera and you can move this using the controls on the bottom left of your screen.

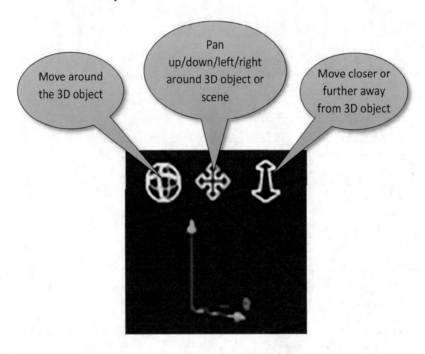

For this demonstration, open the file **3D.psd** in the resources folder for this book.

First, select your move tool from the toolbox on the left-hand side, then click the object you want to have a look at. If you can't click it, select the layer the object is on from the layers panel.

Click the icon, then while holding the button down, move your mouse to adjust your view.

As an example, click and hold your mouse button on the first icon. Now while you're holding your mouse button down, move your mouse up, down, left, and right and see what happens.

Try the other two icons and see what they do.

Inserting 3D Models

You can insert 3D models created in 3Ds or any 3D modeling software. Many of these are available for download on the Internet.

If you haven't already opened a new Photoshop document, do that now. File ➤ New ➤ Select size, for example, A4. Then from the 3D menu, select "New 3d Layer from File."

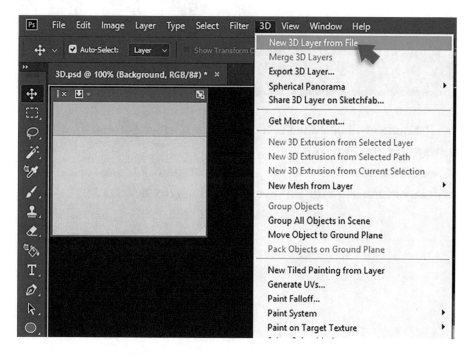

From the dialog box choose a 3D model. There is one included in the resources folder called **spaceshuttleorbiter.3ds** for you to use and experiment with.

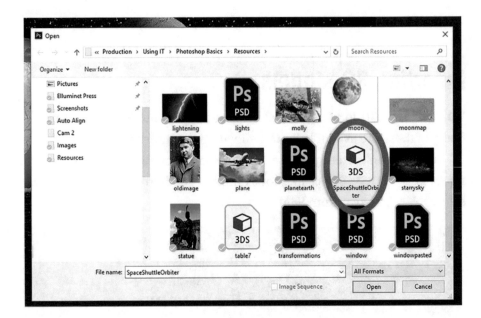

The model will be added as a new 3D layer which you can manipulate, resize, and move into your scene.

Select the size of your scene; your environment. For most of the models, you can leave the settings at their default. Click "OK."

Select your move tool from the toolbox on the top left and click your model.

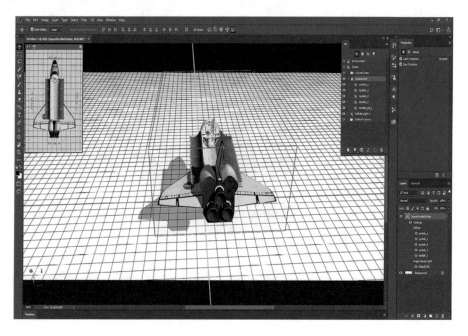

Use the navigation options on the bottom left of the screen to move around your model. Note, this moves your point of view, not the position of the model.

Build Your Scene

You can build up a 3D scene using layers in a similar fashion to 2D projects we have looked at earlier. For this example, open **3D earth.psd**.

We can insert a background. Open your file explorer or finder. Drag and drop **starrysky.jpg** into your project.

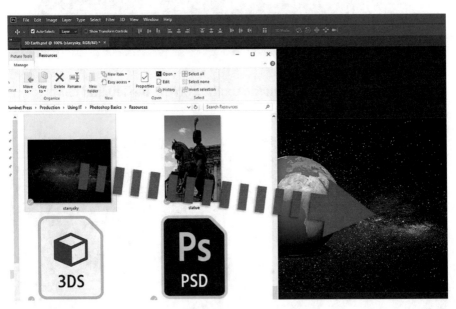

Move the starrysky layer below the earth layer - to put it behind.

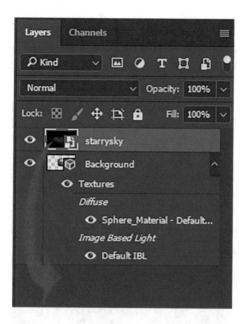

Now, open your file explorer or finder and drag and drop **moonmap. jpg** from the resources folder. Press enter on your keyboard to insert the layer.

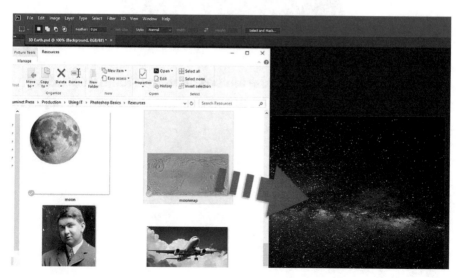

We need to create a 3D object from this layer, so we're going to map the image onto a sphere. From the 3D panel, select "Mesh from Preset" and in the drop down select "Sphere." Hit "Create."

Select your move tool from the toolbox on the left-hand side. Click an object, the moon for example. Use the 3D navigation to move the object in 3D space.

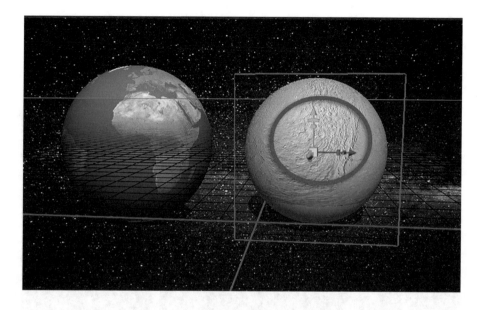

By default, Photoshop adds 3D objects as independent 3D layers. This means they don't interact, cast shadows onto each other, and so on.

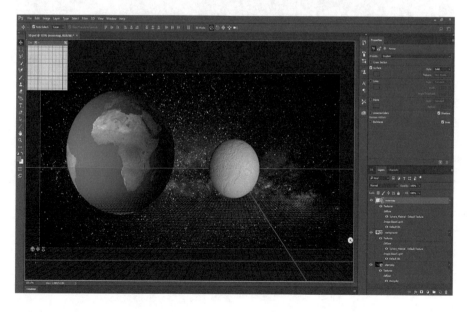

Notice each object in the 3D panel has its own light source and environment - you can adjust the light on each object.

In the following example, the light on the moon isn't casting a shadow on the earth object.

To get objects to interact, you have to merge the layers they're on. For this example, I am going to merge the earth and moon layers. So select both of these in the layers panel. Now go to the 3D menu and select "Merge 3D Layers."

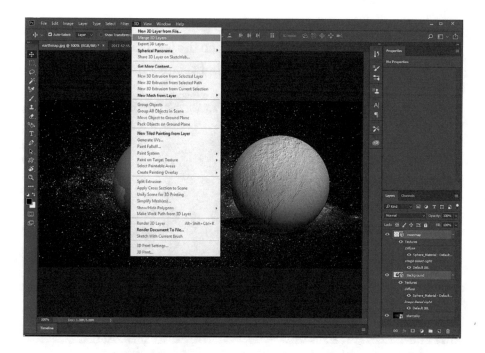

Notice now, there is a shadow on the earth cast by the moon object.

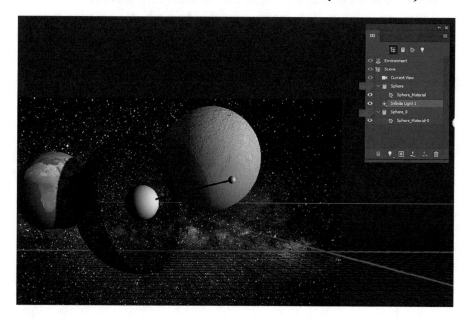

Both the objects now appear in the 3D panel.

Select the move tool from the toolbox on the left-hand side. In the 3D panel, select "Infinite Light 1." This is the light source for these objects.

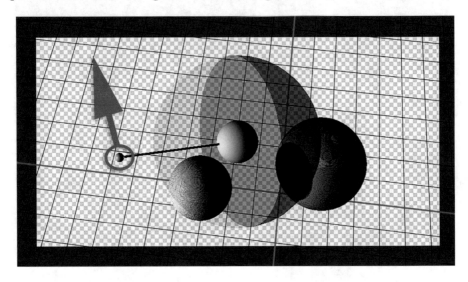

Grab the small ball on the end of the line and drag it around to reposition the light. You'll be able to see the shadows change depending on where you put the light.

You can add more lights. On your 3D panel, click the lightbulb icon on the bottom row.

You can add three types of lights.

- A spotlight provides a very direct source of light.

- A point light emits light in all directions.

- An infinite light shines from one direction similar to sunlight.

Select a "New Spotlight" from the drop-down menu.

Select your move tool from the toolbox on the left-hand side if you haven't already got it selected.

Click "Spotlight" in your 3D panel. This is the light you just created.

On your screen, you'll see two cones emanating from the light source. This is to control the focus of your light beam. Click and drag the handles on the inner cone to adjust the center of the beam and use the outer one to set the focus on a wide area or just a small area.

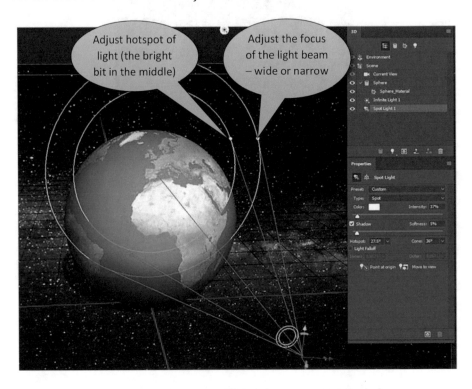

Use the standard 3D handles on the light to move and aim it in your scene.

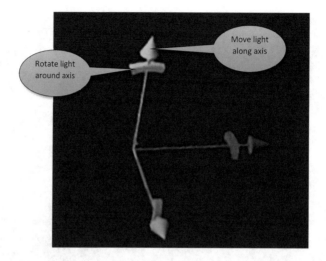

On the properties panel, you can adjust the intensity, type, color, shadow effect, the size of the hotspot in the middle of the light (the bright bit), and the cone to focus the light or widen the light beam.

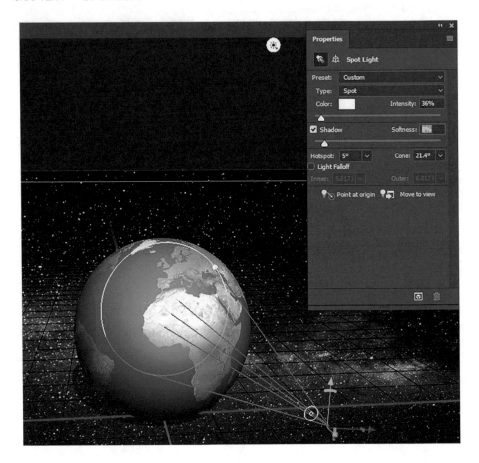

Experiment with some of these settings and see what happens.

Summary

- You can create 3D postcards, extrusions, and meshes.

- You can wrap an image around a 3D object.

- 3D text.

- Insert 3D models.

CHAPTER 8

Introduction to Lightroom Classic

For best results, it is always advisable to shoot your photographs in RAW format, rather than JPG. This allows a lot more flexibility when it comes to post production - adjusting brightness, shadows, contrast, color, and so on.

Think of RAW files along the same lines as a negative as was used in the old film days, or digital negative today. You process your RAW photos then save them out as JPG to use on the web, post on social media, or some design project. This means you always have a copy of your original photograph you can go back to.

There are two applications for storing and editing photos: Lightroom Classic, and Lightroom.

The primary difference is that Lightroom Classic is a full featured desktop-based application and Lightroom is a streamlined cloud-based application available for tablets and phones as well as desktop PCs.

Since we are using a PC (or Mac), we'll be using Lightroom Classic.

Installing Lightroom Classic

To install lightroom classic, open up adobe creative cloud on your start menu.

© Kevin Wilson 2023
K. Wilson, *Introduction to Photoshop*, https://doi.org/10.1007/978-1-4842-8963-1_8

Select "All Apps" on the left-hand side, then select the "Desktop" tab.

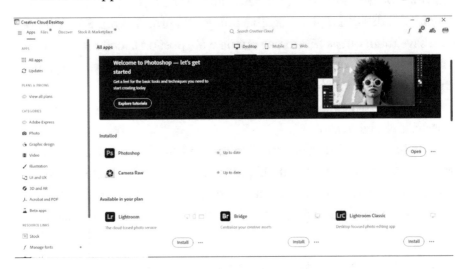

Click "Install" next to "Lightroom Classic."

Allow lightroom classic to install.

Click "Lightroom Classic" on the start menu to launch the app. Or launchpad if you're using a Mac.

Once Lightroom opens, you can select photos, edit them, or import new ones off your camera.

Import Photos

Using Lightroom Classic, connect your camera to your computer, then hit "Import" on the bottom left of the screen.

In the next window, select the photos you want to import. Either click the tick box on the top left of each image you want to import, or click "Import All" if you want to import every photo on your camera.

On the right-hand side, select "Destination," usually "My Catalog." This is the folder on your computer where you want Lightroom classic to store all your photos. Once you're done, click "Import" on the bottom right.

Adjusting Photos

If you want to adjust any image, click the thumbnail. In the following example, I've selected image number 6. Select the "Develop" module on the right-hand side.

Here, you can adjust the brightness, highlights, shadows, and contrast. To do this, select the "basic" folder on the right-hand side. Adjust the sliders. Here in the following example, I've pulled up the shadows.

This works in the same way as the camera raw filter we looked at in Chapter 4. Try some of the other adjustments to see what happens to the image.

Send Image to Photoshop

You can open any image in Photoshop from Lightroom classic. Right-click the image thumbnail, go down to "Edit in," then select "Photoshop...."

If you have adjusted the photograph in Lightroom classic, you may be prompted with a few options. If not, the photo will open up in Photoshop.

If you want Lightroom classic to open the photo with the adjustments you have made, select "Edit a Copy with Lightroom Adjustments." Do not select "Edit Original."

Summary

- You can use adobe bridge or lightroom classic to edit and organize your photographs.

- A histogram shows the tonal range of a photograph - the range of brightness levels from pure black to pure white in the photo.

CHAPTER 9

Digital Images, Resolution, and Color Models

A digital image is an electronic representation of a photograph, image, or artwork encoded in binary and stored on an electronic system such as a computer, tablet, or smartphone.

© Kevin Wilson 2023
K. Wilson, *Introduction to Photoshop*, https://doi.org/10.1007/978-1-4842-8963-1_9

Image Types

There are generally two types of images: bitmap images and vector images.

Bitmap Images

Also known as raster images. These images are made up of thousands of pixels in varying colors and intensities to represent the image. Each pixel has a value, which specifies its color and location.

When you work with bitmap images, you are editing pixels, rather than shapes. This allows for gradations of color and creating a continuous tone appearance.

In the preceding example, because bitmap images contain a fixed number of pixels, they can lose detail or appear jagged edged when they are rescaled on the screen or printed at a higher resolution than they were created for. You can see in the preceding, in the yellow circle, what happens to the image as the size increases - you start to see the pixels.

Vector Images

A vector graphic, on the other hand, is made up of polygons defined by mathematical formulas in 2D or 3D space.

Because of this, you can move, resize, or change the color of the graphic without losing image quality.

This type of graphic is the best choice when you want a logo or bold graphic.

Resolution

Understanding how pixel data is measured and displayed will help you make decisions about your images both when scanning and working with the images in Photoshop.

Image Dimensions

How large an image displays on the computer screen is determined by the pixel dimensions of the image plus the size and setting of the monitor.

On a typical 15″ monitor set to 800x600, an 800x600 image would fill the screen. This same image would fill the screen of a 19″ inch monitor if it were also set to 800x600; each pixel on the 19″ screen would be larger.

Likewise, if the 19″ monitor were set to 1024x768, the image would appear much smaller.

Image Resolution

The number of pixels per inch in an image determines the quality and detail of that image.

Image resolution controls how much space these pixels are spread over when printed or displayed on screen.

A high resolution image contains more and therefore smaller pixels than an image with a low resolution. This means that a 1 inch by 1 inch image at 72 dpi would have 5184 pixels (72x72), whereas the same image at 300 dpi would have 90,000 pixels (300x300).

72 dpi   300 dpi

A higher resolution image produces more detail. However, increasing the resolution of an image only spreads the original pixel information over a larger number of pixels and will not improve image quality.

Most new monitors have a resolution of 96 dpi. No matter how high the resolution may be, we cannot see more than 96 pixels/inch in the displayed picture on a computer.

Printers vary widely; however, your image should always be at least 300dpi if it is to be printed clearly.

Note PPI describes the resolution in pixels of a digital image whereas DPI describes the amount of ink dots on a printed image

Image Compression

High resolution RAW images can be very large without compression, so to save storage space and download times, images are compressed and saved as jpeg, png, or tiff, depending on what they're being used for.

There are two basic types of compression, "Lossy" and "Lossless."

Lossy compression drops unnecessary pixel information from the original file. This is used in jpeg images. A side effect to lossy compression is a loss in quality the more the image is compressed.

Lossless compression retains all the pixel information. This is used in png images.

When working with images, it's best to work on your high resolution master images. These are usually your Photoshop files (PSD files).

The final images should be saved in the appropriate format (.png or .jpeg, .tiff) in a folder called "Images" or "Exports" for the project. This ensures that you will always have your high resolution originals available for future use or if you need to make changes.

You can export as a jpeg or png. To do this, go to the file menu and select "Export," from the slideout, select "Export as."

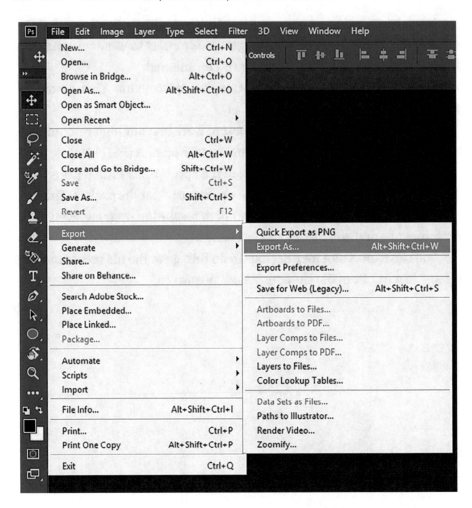

From the dialog box you can select the image format on the top right, use either jpg or png.

For jpg, you can usually leave the quality at 100% for best results; however, if you need to compress the image more, then reduce the quality. The lower this percentage the higher the compression.

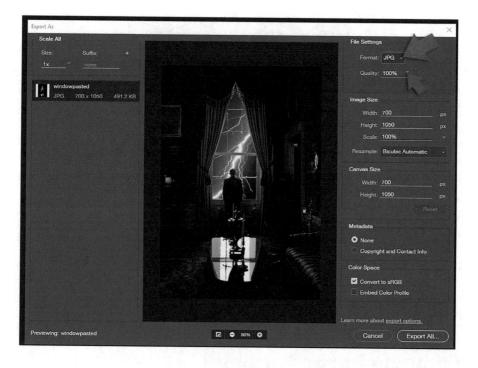

Underneath that, you can set the image size in pixels, or you can resize as a percentage size of the original size - 50% for half the size, 200% for double the size.

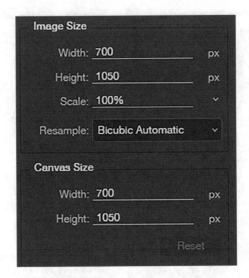

This doesn't alter the compression.

Common Image Formats

There are many different kinds of digital image file formats, each with their own capabilities and restrictions, here is a brief summary of the most common ones.

EPS "Encapsulated PostScript file" - used by programs such as InDesign and Illustrator.

GIF A lossless image compression format, short for "Graphic Interchange Format" and is popular web icons, logos, and buttons, but is limited to 8-bit (256 colors).

JPEG A lossy image compression format short for "Joint Photographic Experts Group" and is a popular format for saving photographs for use on the web or in printing.

PNG An image format using a lossless compression supporting 24-bit images (16.7 million colors) with transparency. This format is usually used on websites.

PSD Photoshop's native multiple layer image format. The format used to save all your multilayer Photoshop projects.

RAW A raw format image is usually a photograph taken using a high-end camera and is best used for high level photography where detail and the ability to adjust image tones and highlights are essential.

TIFF "Tagged Image File Format." These files tend to be either uncompressed or compressed using a lossless compression format and are commonly used in the printing and publishing industry.

Color Models

Commonly used models are RGB and CMYK.

The RGB color model uses the three primary colors red, green, and blue to create various different color variations in an image and is used to display anything on a screen, for example, social media, websites, and photographs.

RGB is known as an additive color model, meaning images are created by mixing red, green, and blue light. Additive colors start with black and the primary colors are added on top of each other in varying intensities to create all the colors you see on screen.

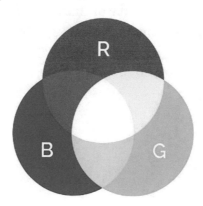

The CMYK color model uses the three primary colors cyan, magenta and yellow to create different color variations in an image and is used to print out anything such as a poster, photograph, or color document. Most printers add a fourth color for black (called key).

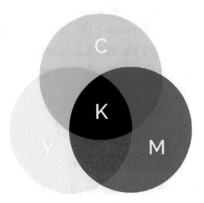

CMYK is known as a subtractive color model as it involves the mixing of cyan, magenta, and yellow ink to create the image on the page. Subtractive colors start with white and the primary colors are added on top of each other in varying intensities to create all the colors in the image on the page.

CMYK is called subtractive because the inks don't emit their own light, instead they subtract (or absorb) the primary colors red, green, and blue from light reflected off the printout to create the colors you see.

You can change the color modes using the "Image" menu. Go down to "Mode," then select either "RGB Color" or "CMYK Color."

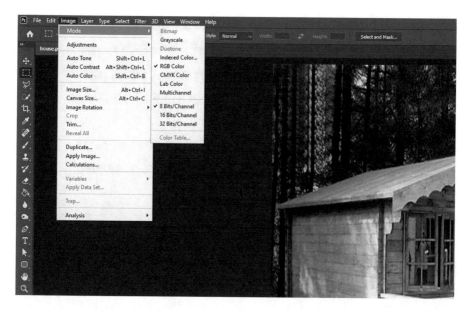

If the final image is to be printed, change the color mode to CMYK. If the final image only appears on a screen, then use RGB.

This is why you'll sometimes notice that the colors in a printout look slightly different to the colors you see on screen.

Summary

- Bitmap Images, also known as raster images, are made up of thousands of pixels in varying colors and intensities.

- A vector graphic is made up of polygons defined by mathematical formulas in 2D or 3D space.

- Image dimension is the size, for example, 800x600 pixels.

- Resolution is the number of pixels per inch and determines the quality and detail of that image.

- RGB is known as an additive color model, and is used to display anything on a screen, such as social media, websites, and photographs.

- CMYK is known as a subtractive color model and is used to print out anything such as a poster, photograph, or color document.

Index

A

B

C

K. Wilson, *Introduction to Photoshop*, https://doi.org/10.1007/978-1-4842-8963-1

Printed in the United States
by Baker & Taylor Publisher Services